JAN HUIZINGA (1872-1945) was educated at the University of Groningen, The Netherlands, and graduated in philology and history. He was *Privaat-docent* of Indian literature at the University of Amsterdam, professor of history at the University of Groningen (1905-1915), and after 1915 professor of general history at the University of Leiden. His books include *Homo Ludens* and *The Waning of the Middle Ages*.

D1287413

IN NORTON PAPERBOUND EDITIONS

Raymond Aron   *On War*   N107
———— *The Opium of the Intellectuals*   N106
Julien Benda   *The Treason of the Intellectuals*   N470
Marc Bloch   *Strange Defeat: A Statement of Evidence Written in 1940*   N371
Jan Huizinga   *In the Shadow of Tomorrow*   N484
John U. Nef   *War and Human Progress: An Essay on the Rise of Industrial Civilization*   N468
José Ortega y Gasset   *The Revolt of the Masses*
Bertrand Russell   *Freedom versus Organization, 1814-1914*   N136
———— *Power*   N479

IN THE SHADOW
OF TOMORROW

BY J. HUIZINGA

Translated from the Dutch by J. H. Huizinga

The Norton Library

W · W · NORTON & COMPANY · INC ·
NEW YORK

Books That Live
The Norton imprint on a book means that in the publisher's
estimation it is a book not for a single season but for the years.
W. W. Norton & Company, Inc.

PRINTED IN THE UNITED STATES OF AMERICA

1 2 3 4 5 6 7 8 9 0

TO
MY CHILDREN

Habet mundus iste noctes suas et non paucas.
—*Saint Bernard*

PREFACE

THIS book is an elaboration of an address delivered at Brussels on March 8th, 1935. It is possible that these pages will lead many to think of me as a pessimist. I have but this to answer: I am an optimist.

J. H.

CONTENTS

CONTENTS

IN THE SHADOW
OF TOMORROW

I

APPREHENSIONS OF DOOM

WE ARE living in a demented world. And we know it. It would not come as a surprise to anyone if tomorrow the madness gave way to a frenzy which would leave our poor Europe in a state of distracted stupor, with engines still turning and flags streaming in the breeze, but with the spirit gone.

Everywhere there are doubts as to the solidity of our social structure, vague fears of the imminent future, a feeling that our civilization is on the way to ruin. They are not merely the shapeless anxieties which beset us in the small hours of the night when the flame of life burns low. They are considered expectations founded on observation and judgment of an overwhelming multitude of facts. How to avoid the recognition that almost all things which once seemed sacred and immutable have now become unsettled, truth and humanity, justice and reason? We see forms of government no longer capable of functioning, production systems on the verge of collapse, social forces gone wild with power. The roaring engine of this tremendous time seems to be heading for a breakdown.

But immediately the antithesis forces itself on our minds. Never has there been a time when men were so clearly conscious of their commanding duty to co-operate in the task of preserving and improving the world's well-being and human civilization. At no time has work been as much honoured as it is to-day. Man was never so ready to apply his full courage and all his powers to a common cause. At least hope has not yet been lost.

If, then, this civilization is to be saved, if it is not to be submerged by centuries of barbarism but to secure the treasures of its inheritance on new and more stable foundations, there is indeed need for those now living fully to realise how far the decay has already progressed.

It is but a little while since the apprehension of impending doom and of a progressive deterioration of civilization has become general. For the majority of men it is the economic crisis with its direct material effects (most of us being more sensitive in body than in spirit), which has first prepared the soil for thoughts and sentiments of this nature. Obviously those whose occupation it is to deal systematically and critically with problems of human society and civilization, philosophers and sociologists, have long ago realised that all was not well with our vaunted modern civilization. They have recognised from the outset that the economic dislocation is only one aspect of a transformation-process of much wider import.

The first ten years of this century have known little if anything in the way of fears and apprehensions regarding the future of our civilization. Friction and threats, shocks and dangers, there were then as ever. But except for the revolution menace which Marxism had hung over the world, they did not appear as evils threatening mankind with ruin, while revolution itself by its adversaries was taken as avoidable and for its advocates promised not destruction but salvation. The *fin-de-siècle* mood of decadence of the nineties had scarcely made itself felt outside the sphere of literary fashion. With the murder of McKinley the anarchism of the deed seemed to have run its course. Socialism appeared to develop into a reform movement. In spite of the Boer War and the Russo-Japanese War the first peace conference could still be thought to have heralded the coming of a new era of international order. The dominant note of political and cultural thought remained one of firm belief that under the supremacy of the white race the world was on the right way to concord and prosperity, safeguarded by a knowledge and power which might well seem to have reached a peak. Concord and prosperity—provided politics marched with reason. But this they failed to do.

It is not to the War years that we must look to find the turning of the tide. Then all attention was absorbed in the immediate preoccupation. For many the first few years after the War were filled with optimistic expectations of a new redeeming internationalism. The swift rising but ill-founded trade boom which was to break in 1929 delayed the emergence of a widespread feeling of pessimism for a little longer.

To-day, however, the sense of living in the midst of a violent crisis of civilization, threatening complete collapse, has spread far and wide. Oswald Spengler's *Untergang des Abendlandes* * has been the alarm signal for untold numbers the world over. This is not to say that all those who have read Spengler's famous work have become converts to his views. But it has jolted them out of their unreasoning faith in the providential nature of Progress and familiarised them with the idea of a decline of existing civilization and culture in our own time. Unperturbed optimism is at present only possible for those who through lack of insight fail to realise what is ailing civilization, having themselves been affected by the disease, and for those who in their social or political creed of salvation think to have the key to the hidden treasure-room of earthly weal from which to scatter on humanity the blessings of the civilization to come.

Between the extremes of despairing pessimism and

* English translation: *The Decline of The West;* New York: Alfred A. Knopf.

the belief in imminent deliverance stand all those who see the grave evils and shortcomings of our time, who do not know how they are to be remedied and overcome, but who hope and work, who strive to understand and are ready to bear.

II

NEW FEARS AND OLD

THE question may be raised whether the gravity of the present crisis is not often over-estimated just because of the fact that its portent is so clearly realised. Earlier periods of dangerous tension knew next to nothing of economics, sociology or psychology. They also missed the immediate and far-reaching publicity of all the world's day-to-day happenings. We, in our time, however, see every tear in the tissue and hear every cracking of the joints. Our exact and many-sided information renders us fully aware of the extreme instability of the structure of society and as such of the absolute "dangerousness" of the situation. Not only has our range of anticipation grown much wider, but also, through the field-glasses of our multiform knowledge, we perceive the figures on this range with alarming clarity.

It will be useful, therefore, to orientate our crisis-consciousness historically through a comparison with the great disturbances of older times. At once a very essential difference between past and present is disclosed. The feeling that the world, however small or large, is in danger, that it is threatened with decay or collapse, has been alive in many periods. Usually, however, such fears were part of the eschatological expectation of the coming of the end of all things. Hence the thought of how to avert the evil did not arise. A systematic formulation of the crisis-consciousness of earlier times was *a priori* out of the question. It was essentially of a religious nature. In so far as the anticipation of approaching doom and judgment left room for terrestrial anxieties, these remained suspended in an atmosphere of vague fear which, to a certain extent, discharged itself in hate of the mighty to whom the earthly miseries were attributed, whether these were held to be the wicked in general, or the heretics, the witches and sorcerers, the rich, the king's counsellors, the aristocrats, the Jesuits, the freemasons, with the choice always depending on the particular attitude of the period. In wide circles the reappearance of crude and low standards of judgment has revived the phantasms of such organised satanic forces. Even educated people to-day frequently indulge in the sort of malignant judgment which would hardly be excusable in the meanest and most ignorant rabble.

Not always, however, did the contemplation of the future and the deprecation of the present wholly resolve themselves in visions of a coming doom and eternal retribution. At several periods in history the promise of a bright future replacing the evil present has filled the spirit with glad hopes. But here also there is a difference with the mentality of our time. The coming happiness seemed always close at hand, within reach as it were. To recognise the error of our ways, to overcome a mistaken belief and to revert to virtue was all that was needed. The change was seen as an imminent revulsion.

Thus it was seen by every religious teaching which preached peace on earth as well as everlasting salvation. And thus Erasmus saw it. With the rediscovery of the ancient learning the way had been cleared to the pure sources of the Faith. There was no longer anything to delay the attainment of such a degree of earthly perfection as the order of things allowed. Concord, humanity and civilization would presently spring from the newly gained insight. To the Age of Reason and Rousseau the world's well-being similarly seemed to turn on insight and the following of its dictates. For the former these were the discarding of superstition and the triumph of knowledge, for the latter the return to nature and the practice of virtue. From this age-old and constantly renewed representation of a simple revulsion or reversion of society arose the concept of Revolution. The term revolution was derived from the rotation of a wheel. In the background of the image stood always the Wheel of Fortune. In the political sense the term remains at first limited to simple and direct turnings such as that of 1688. It is not until after the great event of 1789 that the concept of revolution in the course of the nineteenth century comes to be charged with all the significance which socialism was to give it. Revolution as an ideal concept always preserves the essential content of the original thought: sudden and lasting betterment.

24

This time-honoured representation of an abrupt and consciously desired revulsion of society is one which the mind of our time, with its modern well-founded knowledge which considers all that is of nature and man as the product of numberless interdependent long-term forces, refuses to accept. In the process of interacting social forces our mind sees the action of the human will as a factor of only limited significance without thereby professing adherence to a rigid determinism. Grouping himself efficiently and using his energies to best advantage man can avail himself of the natural and social forces which govern the dynamic processes of society. He can influence certain tendencies of the process, but he cannot alter its main direction. This conviction of the "Irreversibility" of the social process has found its formal expression in the word Evolution. It is a concept which contains its own contradiction but which has nevertheless become indispensable as an intellectual instrument of a rather crude sort. Evolution means limited necessity; it stands in direct opposition to Revulsion, Revolution. In contrast with the naïve expectations of earlier times which saw the approach of the end of all things or of a golden age, our thinking is founded in the steady conviction that the crisis through which we are passing is a phase in a progressive irreversible sequence. Whatever our creed or our belief, we all know that there is no way back, that we must fight our way *through*. This is the entirely new feature of the crisis-consciousness of our time.

The third contrast between earlier apprehensions of decline and those of the present is already implicit in the one just mentioned. All through history the heralds of better things and times to come, reformers, prophets, the bearers and champions of renaissances, restorations or *réveils,* have always pointed to past glories and urged a return to and a retrieval of ancient purity. The Humanists, the Reformers and the moralists of Roman times, Rousseau, Mohammed, even the prophets of a Central African negro tribe, ever had before their eyes the haunting vision of an illusory past of finer quality than the gross present. And it was to this past that they exhorted mankind to return.

We in our time neither ignore nor depreciate past glories. We know that at many periods many things

26

have been better than they are to-day. Possibly certain particular relationships may one day reapproach older and more desirable forms. But we know: a general going *back* is out of the question. There is nothing but to go forward even if we stand appalled at the unknown depths and distances ahead, even if the near future faces us as a yawning abyss shrouded in dark impenetrable vapours.

III

THE PRESENT CRISIS COMPARED WITH
THOSE OF THE PAST

Is it possible to find historical examples of the civilization of a nation, an empire or a continent, passing through as violent a convulsion as that which racks our time? Crisis of civilization is an historical concept. Through historical appreciation, through a comparison of past and present, the concept can be given a certain degree of objectivity. For of the earlier crises we not only know the origins and development but also the consummation. Our knowledge of them has an additional dimension. Sometimes an entire civilization perished, sometimes it won its way through to new and different forms of existence. We are able to view the historical case as a closed process. And although such historical autopsy of the past does not hold out the promise of a cure for the present and perhaps not even that of a prognosis, no possible method to gain an insight into the nature of the ailment may be left untried.

Unfortunately the material of comparable cases is rather less plentiful than it might seem at first. However telling the remains of the many civilizations which are daily made to emerge from under the desert sand, tropical vegetation, or the wastes of depopulated regions, we know far too little of their internal history to be able to discern other causes of their decline and downfall than catastrophes of some sort. Even ancient Greece and Egypt afford hardly any material for an accurate comparison. The twenty centuries since the reign of Augustus and the life of Christ alone are sufficiently near to us to allow of fruitful comparison.

It may be asked: has not civilization during these twenty centuries always been in a state of crisis? Is not all mankind's history precarious to the utmost degree? To be sure, but this is wisdom for philosophical declamation, useful on the proper occasion. Viewed historically, however, certain complexes of past events do present themselves as more or less clearly marked-out periods of intensive cultural change. They are: the transition from Antiquity to the Middle Ages; from the Middle Ages to Modern times; and that from the eighteenth to the nineteenth century.

Consider first the period around 1500. The time is one of tremendous changes; the earth discovered in all its fullness, the structure of the planetary system revealed, the Church torn asunder, the power and the range of the written word infinitely extended by the printing press, the means of warfare vastly augmented, credit and finance growing abundantly, Greek learning restored, the old architecture scorned, the arts unfolding in all their splendour. Then look at 1789–1815. Again the current of the world's happenings has swollen to a roaring torrent. The first state of Europe succumbed to the delusions of the "philosophers" and the fury of the mob, but presently resurrected by the deeds and fortune of a military genius. Liberty acclaimed and the Church doctrines forsaken. The Continent of Europe thrown into a jumble and finally put together again. Steam engines panting and the crashing rhythm of the new weaving looms. One scientific conquest after another, the world of the spirit enriched by German philosophy and life's charm enhanced by German music. America politically and economically grown-up, culturally still a youngster.

At both times history's seismograph seems to register as violent a disturbance as to-day. On the surface the shocks, the landslides, and the tidal waves seem to be no less powerful in their effects than those of the present. Probing deeper, however, it soon appears that in both of the earlier critical periods, that of Renaissance and Reformation and that of Revolution and Napoleon, the foundations of society have been less convulsed than in our time. And more important, in both the earlier periods hope and faith remained far more dominant than to-day. Even though then, too, there were many who in the passing of the old and cherished order saw the coming of the end, the feeling of a threatening collapse of all civilization was then neither so widespread nor so strongly founded on exact observation. To the historical eye both periods, however critical, bear above all the mark of ascent.

To repeat, around 1500 and again around 1800 the

foundations of society have been much less shaken than to-day. Fiercely as the Catholic and the Protestant world after the Reformation hated and fought one another, the common base of their faith and their Churches kept them much more closely related and rendered the breach with the past much less definite than in our time with its cleft between the absolute rejection of religious belief on the one hand and the reconstitution of Christian faith on the old foundations on the other. Apart from certain fantastical excesses, neither the sixteenth century nor the revolutionary era has deliberately attacked or disavowed the Christian system of morals. The changes of the political structure in the period 1789–1815, including all the successive phases of the French Revolution, are far less fundamental than those that have occurred since 1914, while in the sixteenth century the political structure remained virtually unaffected. Neither the sixteenth century nor the first decades of the nineteenth century have known the systematic undermining of the social order by a creed of class struggle and class antagonism. The economy of both periods, while bearing the mark of crisis, fails to show signs of thorough dislocation. The great economic shifts of the sixteenth century, the virulence of capitalism, the great bankruptcies and the rise of prices, never brought on the convulsed paralysis of trade or the wild currency disorders of the present. The confusion caused by the assignats towards the end of the eighteenth century is as nothing compared to the endless monetary ills of our time. Even the so-called Industrial Revolution (the fitness of the term is questionable) was not of the nature of a violent disturbance but of excessive one-sided growth.

If still another sensitive test is wanted to expose the febrile character of the cultural life of our time, consider the course of the arts. All the transitions through which they have passed, from the Quattrocento to Rococo, have been gradual and conservative. During all this time schooling and craftsmanship remained the unquestioningly accepted prerequisites of all true art. Not until the advent of Impressionism does the repudiation of principles set in which opened the way for the burlesque parade of the fashionable and publicity-crazed modernities of our century.

The comparison of the present with the time of 1500 and 1800, then, gives rise to the general impression that the world is now in the throes of a more intense and more fundamental upheaval than at either of the earlier periods.

There remains the question in how far the process through which we are passing resembles that of the transition from Roman civilization to the Middle Ages. Here indeed we see what many now think close at hand: a high and rich civilization gradually ceding to another of unmistakably lower quality and equipment. But at once a great difference between the two cases appears. The lower civilization of about A.D. 500 had emerged out of the older one carrying with it the treasure of the high form of religion on which in a way the old civilization itself had foundered. With all its barbarian qualities this age of Gregory the Great and the Merovingians was permeated with an intense metaphysical element. Christianity, in spite of its renunciation of the world, has been the propelling force in the development of mediæval culture to the high and harmonious form in which the twelfth and thirteenth centuries displayed it.

Is this same force of Christian faith acting as powerfully for the future in our time?

Apart from the triumph of Christianity, the cultural transformations of the Roman Empire appear to us as a process of stagnation and degeneration. We see high faculties of social organisation and intellectual encompassment and expression shrinking, withering, and dissolving. There was a declining efficiency of government, technology at a standstill, diminishing productivity, and slackening of intellectual curiosity and construction which remained largely confined to preservation and imitation. In all these aspects the development of Roman civilization bears little resemblance to the processes of our time. For to-day most of the above-mentioned faculties still seem to be steadily growing in intensity, diversity and refinement. The general conditions are, moreover, altogether different. Then there was a multiplicity of peoples loosely, imperfectly, and yet truly held together in one world-state. To-day we live in a very tightly linked structure of separate competing states. In our world technical ability reigns ever more unchallenged, productive capacity continues to expand, and the power of scientific research triumphs in a seemingly unending succession of new discoveries. Again, the pace of the process of change is an entirely different one; years seem to have replaced centuries as the yardstick of measurement. Briefly, comparison with the history of A.D. 200–600 offers too few points of contact to be of immediate value for an understanding of our present crisis.

And yet, despite all differences, one important point stands out. The road of Roman civilization was a road to barbarism. Will it turn out to be the same road we are on to-day?

Whatever historical comparison may afford for an understanding of the present crisis, it can give us no assurance regarding the latter's outcome. The confident conclusion that things will right themselves somehow is not warranted by any historical parallel. We continue to push on into the unknown.

In this aspect also our time presents an important difference from earlier periods of violent cultural turmoil. In these earlier periods men have always seen the aim for which to strive and the means with which to pursue it, as fixed and positively determined. As we have said before, their aim was almost always to *restore;* a return to old perfection and purity. The ideal was retrospective. And not only the ideal but also the method by which to realise it. It lay in the acquisition and application of *ancient* wisdom and *ancient* virtue. The ancient wisdom, the ancient beauty, the ancient virtue, these were the wisdom, the beauty, and the virtue needed to bring to this world the order and serenity which earthly conditions allow. In dark times of decline the noblest spirits—think of a Boëthius—used to conserve the ancestral wisdom to pass it on to the coming generations for their guidance and instruction. Well may they be thankful for it; without Boëthius what would the Dark Ages have been? In rising times the lost wisdom was unearthed, not for the sake of disinterested knowledge alone, but to turn it to practical use; Roman Law, Aristotle. Thus Humanism in the fifteenth and sixteenth centuries spread before the world the rediscovered treasures of a purified antiquity as the everlasting model of knowledge and culture, a model to build on if not to swear by. Practically all conscious cultural striving of earlier periods has in one way or another been inspired with the principle of an exemplary past.

Such veneration of the past we no longer know. Where our time seeks, preserves, safeguards ancient beauty, wisdom and greatness, it does not do so, at least not in the first place, with the object of finding guidance. Even though we may rate older periods higher than the present, for their faith, their art and the solidity and soundness of their social forms, our cultural life is no longer directed towards the illusory ideal of reinstatement. We are neither able nor willing to look back. For us there are only the unknown distances ahead. For three centuries, since Bacon and Descartes, our face has been turned to the future. Humanity has to find its own way. The impulse to push on ever further can lead to extremes when it degenerates into a vain and restless hankering after novelty for the sake of novelty itself. The stronger spirits, however, do not fear a heavy load of ancient values in their onward stride.

We know it only too well: if we are to preserve culture we must continue to create it.

IV

FUNDAMENTALS OF CULTURE

WHAT do we mean by Culture? The word has emanated from Germany. It has long since been accepted by the Dutch, the Scandinavian and the Slavonic languages, while in Spain, Italy, and America it has also achieved full standing. Only in French and English does it still meet with a certain resistance in spite of its currency in some well-defined and traditional meanings. At least it is not unconditionally interchangeable with civilization in these two languages. This is no accident. Because of the old and abundant development of their scientific vocabulary, French and English had far less need to rely on the German example for their modern scientific nomenclature than most other European languages, which throughout the nineteenth century fed in increasing degree on the rich table of German phraseology.

Oswald Spengler posited the terms culture and civilization as the poles of his sharply pointed but all too dogmatic decline-theory. The world has read him and heard his warning words, but it has not been able to accept either his terminology or his judgment.

In general usage the word culture is not apt to create misunderstanding. One knows more or less what is meant by it. To give an accurate description of its meaning, however, is a different thing altogether. What is culture, what does it consist of? An exhaustive definition is practically impossible. All we can do is to enumerate a few essential conditions and requirements without which there can be no such thing as culture.

Culture requires in the first place a certain balance of material and spiritual values. This permits the emergence of a social condition which is appreciated by those living in it as affording more and higher values than the mere gratification of want and the desire for power. These values lie in the domain of the spiritual, the intellectual, the moral, and the æsthetic. These several domains themselves must again be in balance and harmony to render the concept of culture applicable. By stressing equilibrium and not absolute level one is enabled to include early or low or crude forms of society in a cultural evaluation, and to avoid the danger of over-estimating the highly refined civilizations and of one-sided appreciation of one of the several factors of culture, be it religion, art, law, political organisation or any other. This equilibrium may be viewed as a harmonious and energetic functioning of the several cultural activities within the whole. The result of such co-ordination of the cultural activities manifests itself in order, structural strength, and rhythm of the particular society. It is clear that the historical evaluation of different cultures, no more than the appreciation of present environment, can free itself from the preconceived standards of the judging subject. In this connection it must be noted that the general qualification of a culture as a "high" or "low" culture appears ultimately to be determined by its spiritual and ethical rather than its intellectual and æsthetic value content. A culture which does not boast tech-

nical achievements or great sculptural art may still
be a high culture, but not if it lacks charity.

The second fundamental feature of culture is that
all culture has an element of striving. It is directed
towards an aim and this aim is always an ideal, not
the ideal of an individual, but an ideal for society.
The nature of this ideal varies greatly. It may be
purely spiritual: celestial bliss, nearness to God, lib-
eration from earthly ties; or: knowledge, rational or
mystical, knowledge of nature, knowledge of self
and the mind, knowledge of the divine. It may be a
social ideal: honour, respect, power, greatness, but
always honour, respect, power and greatness for the
community. Again, it may be economic or hygienic:
prosperity or health. For the bearers of culture the
ideal always means betterment or weal, weal here or
elsewhere, now or later.

Whether the aim is in heaven or on earth, wisdom
or wealth, the essential condition of its pursuit and
attainment is always security and order. Culture
could not be a striving if it did not first of all fulfil
the imperative task of maintaining security and order. From the requirement of order springs all that

is authority, from that of security all that is law. At the bottom of scores of different systems of law and government there are always the social groupings whose striving for betterment gives rise to culture.

More concrete and more positive than the first-mentioned fundamentals of culture, balance and striving, is the third, chronologically its first and most typical feature. Culture means control over nature. Culture exists the moment man discovers that the hand armed with the flint is capable of things which without it would have been beyond his reach. He has bent a part of nature to his will. He controls nature, his enemy and his benefactor. He has acquired instruments, means; he has become *homo faber*. He uses these means to gratify a want, to construct an implement, to protect himself and his kin, to destroy animal or foe. Henceforward he changes the course of nature, for the results of his handling the tool would not have occurred without it.

If this control over nature were the only prerequisite of culture there would be little reason to deny ants, bees, birds or beavers the claim to its possession.

They all turn parts of nature to their use by altering them. Whether or not these activities include a striving for betterment is a question for animal psychology to answer. But even if they did, the attribution of culture to the animal world would still meet with the spontaneous reaction that this is abusing the term. The spirit cannot be eliminated quite as easily as some would think.

In fact, to say that culture is control over nature in the sense of building, shooting and roasting is to tell only half the story. The rich word "nature" includes human nature as well and that also must be controlled. Already in the earliest and simplest phases of society man becomes conscious that he owes something. The animal's care and defence of his young are not sufficient to warrant the conclusion that there too this consciousness exists. It is only in the human consciousness that the function of caring and providing takes on the aspect of Duty. The recognition of this duty is only in a relatively small degree attributable to natural circumstances such as motherhood and protection of the family unit. At an early stage of social organisation the obligation expands into conventions, rules of conduct and cults, in the form of *taboos*. In wide circles the popularisation of the word *taboo* has led to an undervaluation of the ethical element of the so-called primitive cultures, not to say anything of that body of sociological thought which with truly modern simplicity disposes of everything called morality, law, or piety, as just so many *taboos*.

The consciousness of owing something contains an ethical element as soon as there is no absolute material necessity to honour what is felt as an obligation to a fellow-man, an institution or a spiritual power. Ethnologists like Malinowski have shown that the view that in primitive civilizations obedience to the social code is mechanically determined and inescapable, is untenable. Whenever in a community the rules of social conduct are generally observed, therefore, it is through the operation of a genuine ethical impulse. The requirement of control over nature in the form of domination of human nature itself is then fulfilled.

The more the specific feelings of being under obligation range themselves under a supreme principle of human dependence the clearer and the more fertile will be the realisation of the concept, indispensable to all true culture, of service; from the service of God down to the simple social relationship as between employer and employee. The uprooting and discrediting of the service-concept has been the most destructive function of the shallow rationalism of the eighteenth century.

Were we now to sum up what we have set out above as the essential features and general requirements of culture, the contents of this concept might perhaps be formulated in the following statement, which cannot lay any claim to the quality of exact definition, however. Culture, as a condition of society, is present when the control over nature in the material, the moral, and spiritual field maintains a state which is *higher* and *better* than would follow from the given natural conditions, and whose characteristics are a harmonious balance of material and spiritual values and a more or less homogeneous ideal in whose pursuit the community's various activities converge.

If the foregoing description—from which the valuation higher and better with its subjective tinge can-

46

not be eliminated—contains a certain amount of truth, the question now arises whether in our time the essential conditions of culture are present.

Culture presupposes control over nature. This condition does, indeed, seem to have found a greater degree of fulfilment than in any known civilization of the past. Forces whose existence was hardly guessed at a century ago and whose character and possibilities were completely unknown, have been harnessed in a thousand ways with effects in the heights and the depths undreamt of a generation earlier. Nor is the end of this march of conquest yet in sight. Hardly a year passes without the discovery of new forces of nature and the means to turn them to advantage.

Physical nature lies at our feet shackled with a hundred chains. What of the control of human nature? Do not point to the triumphs of psychiatry, social services, or the war against crime. Domination of human nature can only mean the domination of every man by himself. Has he achieved this? Or, perfection being beyond his reach, does his domination of himself bear any proportion to his vastly increased control over physical nature? There is hardly reason to think so. Only too often it seems as if man, abusing the freedom obtained through his control over physical nature, refuses to dominate himself and is ready to abdicate all the values which the spirit had gained him. The rights and claims of human nature are everywhere called upon to question the authority of absolute ethical laws. The condition, control over nature, is only halfway fulfilled.

For the fulfilment of the second condition of culture, the pursuit of a largely homogeneous ideal, everything is lacking. The desire for betterment driving every community and every individual looks through a hundred different eyes. Every group pursues its own particular conception of weal without integrating it in one all-embracing ideal superimposed on the various particular desires. It is only the expression of such a common ideal, whether attainable or illusory, which could afford full justification for the term *"our* culture." In older times we do find such common ideals: the glory of God, however understood, justice, virtue, wisdom. Obsolete metaphysical conceptions, the spirit of to-day will object. But with the abandonment of such conceptions the homogeneity of culture is in jeopardy. For what re-places these high principles of action is then nothing but a conglomeration of conflicting desires. The factors linking the cultural aims of our time together can only be found in the series prosperity, power and security (security, because it includes peace and order as well), all ideals which are more apt to divide than to unite and all springing directly from natural instincts, untouched by the spirit. Even the cave-dweller knew them thousands of years ago.

Now one hears a great deal to-day of "national cultures" and "class cultures," that is to say, the con-cept culture is made subservient to the power, pros-perity, or security ideal of a particular group. Those doing so, however, deprive the concept of all its real meaning; for they forget the paradoxical but, in view of the foregoing, inescapable conclusion that one can only speak of culture when the ideal dominating it transgresses the interests of the community claim-ing the possession of culture. Culture must have its ultimate aim in the metaphysical or it will cease to be culture.

Can the world of to-day claim that balance of spiritual and material values which we took to be a prerequisite of culture? Again, the answer must be largely negative. There is intensive production in both fields, certainly, but—balance? Harmony and equipollence of material and spiritual power?

The manifestations of our time all around us seem to exclude every thought of a true equilibrium. A highly refined economic system daily puts forth a mass of products and sets forces in motion which nobody wants and which bring advantage to none, which everyone fears, which many scorn as unworthy, absurd and mischievous. Coffee is burnt to maintain its market, war material finds eager buyers but no one desires that it be used. The disproportion between the perfection and capacity of the productive apparatus and the power to turn it to advantage, poverty in the midst of plenty: they all leave little room for the idea of equilibrium. There is intellectual over-production as well, a permanent surfeit of the written and the "wireless" word and a well-nigh hopeless divergence of thought. Art has been caught in the vicious circle which chains the artist to publicity and through it to fashion, both of which are again dependent on commercial interests. Throughout the whole range, from the life of the State to the life of the family, a dislocation seems to be in process such as the world has never known before. Of true equilibrium, of balance, there can be no question.

V

THE PROBLEMATIC NATURE OF PROGRESS

BEFORE we enquire closer into the various manifestations of the cultural crisis, it seems desirable to pause on a different note from that of well-nigh despairing gloom.

Our judgment of human affairs and relations can never free itself entirely from the mood of the moment. If it is a negative mood there is an objective probability that it will colour our views a shade too dark. If we are in the habit of viewing past epochs, Hellas in the days of Pericles, the age of the cathedrals or the Renaissance, in the light of harmony and equilibrium while our own time appears full of friction and disturbance, this is no doubt partly because of the soothing effect of remoteness. We must at once, before we consider the symptoms, allow for a margin of error, therefore. There can be no perfect balance of our cool vision of the distant past and our troubled view of a present in which we are ourselves concerned. Perhaps a final retrospective judgment of our time will see the phenomena which now cause us such anxiety as of only passing and superficial importance. An insignificant disturbance may rob one of sleep and appetite, spoil one's temper and hinder one's work while the organism is sound and untouched. Signs are not altogether wanting that beneath all the social and cultural afflictions with which we are plagued, the pulse of society nevertheless continues to beat more vigorously and healthily than we realise. But that there is disease and that the organism does not function normally is certain.

Here we find ourselves carrying on the argument in medical metaphors. Without metaphor the handling of general concepts such as culture and civilization becomes impossible, and that of disease and disorder is the obvious one for the case in point. Is not crisis itself a concept we owe to Hippocrates? In the social and cultural domain no metaphor is more apt than the pathological one. No doubt our time is full of fever. Growing pains? Possibly. There is raving, wild phantasms and senseless expression. Or is it more than a passing over-stimulation of the brain? Is there reason to speak of a derangement caused by a serious lesion of the nerve centre? Every one of these metaphors has its weight of meaning when applied to the aspects of the present state of our culture.

Most visible and most tangible are the disturbances of the economic organism. Everyone feels them daily in his own life. Those of the body politic are only slightly less direct, though the average person observes their presence and effects in general only through the medium of the press. Viewing the political and economic dislocation and its gradual progress as a whole, it seems to come down to this. The world's equipment has been perfected to a point where the social forces, uncontrolled and unco-ordinated by a principle which transgresses the particular purpose of each one of these forces (for the State cannot be considered as such), function each separately with an excess of power which is distinctly harmful to the harmony of the organism as a whole. Equipment here refers to the means of production and technical means in general, the means of communication and transport, of publicity and mass-mobilisation, including education and political organisation.

When one considers the development of each one of these means by itself without introducing a valuation, this development fully warrants the application of the term progress. They have all increased enormously in power. Remember, however, that progress in itself merely indicates a direction without implying anything as to where the road leads, whether to salvation or perdition. We are too apt to forget that alone the shallow optimism of our ancestors of the eighteenth and nineteenth centuries has confused the assurance of the bigger and *better* with the purely directional conception of "further." The expectation that every new discovery or refinement of existing means must contain the promise of higher value or greater happiness is an extremely naïve thought, heirloom of the charming age of intellectual, moral and sentimental optimism. It is not in the least paradoxical to say that a culture may founder on real and tangible progress. William James once said: "Progress is a terrible thing." It is more than that: it is also a highly ambiguous notion. For who knows but that a little further on the way a bridge may not have collapsed or a crevice split the earth?

VI

SCIENCE AT THE LIMITS OF THINKING POWER

THE domain of science is the natural starting-point for a description of the outward manifestations of the cultural disorder. For there we find combined unmistakable and steady progress, an equally unmistakable appearance of crisis and an unshaken belief that to preserve and to continue is both imperative and beneficial.

Ever since the seventeenth century the development of scientific and philosophical thought bears the clear mark of positive and uninterrupted progress. Practically every branch of knowledge, philosophy not excluded, is still daily being refined and extended. Astounding discoveries—think only of cos-

mic radiation or positive electrons—follow one another in close succession. This progress is most evident in the natural sciences, especially because of the
immediate technical application of the new discoveries. But also the social sciences and the humanities,
as well as the two branches of knowledge which
stand apart from all others, mathematics and philosophy, are continuously penetrating ever deeper into
the mine of knowledge with ever more refined means
of observation and expression.

All this is the more striking when one remembers
that the generation of about the period 1890 believed
that science had well-nigh reached a point where it
could go no further. The structure of human knowledge appeared to be almost completed. There was
still a little polishing and finishing to be done and
the march of time might bring some new material,
but fundamental changes in the constitution and
formulation of our knowledge were apparently not
to be expected. How very differently it would turn
out! Were a scientific Epimenides who had moved
into his cave in 1879 and slept his eight times seven
years there, to wake up to-day, even the language
of almost all branches of science would have become

incomprehensible to him. The terminology of physics, chemistry, philosophy, psychology, or linguistics,
to mention but a few, would be a meaningless jumble
to him. Anyone surveying the nomenclature of his
intellectual domain realises at once that he is constantly using words and notions which forty years
ago did not exist. If some fields of knowledge
such as history constitute an exception in this respect,
it is because there the terms of everyday life must
generally continue to be the only medium of expression.

When one now compares the present state of all
knowledge with that of fifty years ago the conclusion can be no other than that its progress has been
synonymous with improvement. Our knowledge
has become more extensive as well as deeper and
finer. In terms of value there has been a definite increase. This leads directly to a surprising conclusion;
on the way of real positive progress the mind neither
can nor will ever turn back. The idea that a scientific
thinker would willingly renounce all that has been
gained through new conquests is absurd, while in
the arts, on the other hand, where there is no progressive development in a continuous series, it is

quite conceivable that one might want to forget the progress of an entire period. It has happened often enough.

The example of science, then, shows us a highly important field of culture where at least up to the present the progression is unmistakable and, to all appearances, unbroken. It is a field where the spirit finds its way clearly and definitely marked. Whither it will lead us and what the promise which motions us onward, it is not for us to know.

One thing is certain. This undeniable and positive progress, by which I mean penetration, refinement, purification, in short, improvement, has brought scientific thinking to a state of crisis the outcome of which still remains shrouded in uncertainty. The new knowledge has not yet settled in culture. It has not yet been integrated in a new cosmic conception of illuminating harmony. The aggregate of all knowledge has not yet become culture in us. Rather it would seem as if, with the progressive scientific penetration and dissection of reality, the foundations of our thinking grow ever more precarious and unstable. Old truths have to be abandoned, general terms of everyday use which we thought to be the keys to understanding will now no longer fit the lock. Evolution, yes, but be very careful with it, for the concept is slightly rusty. Elements . . . their immutability no longer exists. Causation . . . on the whole there is little one can do with the concept; it breaks at the slightest usage. Natural laws . . . certainly, but better not talk too much of absolute validity. Objectivity . . . it is still our duty as well as our ideal, but its perfect realisation is not possible, at least not for the social sciences and the humanities.

Our Epimenides of a moment ago may well heave sighs of despair at all this. How he will rub his eyes in incredulous wonder when told that in some sciences (it is said of mathematics) analysis has become so diversified and refined that even the closest professional colleagues can no longer fully understand one another. How great will be his joyful surprise, on the other hand, at hearing that the homogeneity of all matter is on the point of being proved, so that chemistry will have to return to the lap of physics from which once it sprang.

But then again there is this: the means of apperception themselves are beginning to fail us. In the field of microphysics the phenomena must begin to escape observation, since the processes under investigation are more delicate than the instruments of observation, limited as the latter's capacities are by the speed of light. In the case of the most minute quantities the disturbance of the process caused by the fact of observation itself is such as to render full objectivity unattainable. Causation then comes to the border-line of its validity behind which there lies a field of undetermined occurrence.

The phenomena which physics embodies in exact formulæ are so remote from our plane of life, the relationships established in mathematics lie so far beyond the sphere in which our thinking moves, that both sciences have long since felt themselves forced to recognise the insufficiency of our old and seemingly well-tested logical instrument. We have had to familiarise ourselves with the idea that for an understanding of nature one may have to work with non-Euclidian geometry and more than three dimensions. Reason in its old form, wedded as it is to Aristotelian logic, can no longer keep up with science. Research forces us to think far beyond the limits of the imagination. Formulæ afford the medium of expressing the new discoveries, but the imagination is incapable of conveying the particular reality to our mind. The confident "it is" is reduced to a hesitating "it appears to be." A process appears to be the action of waves or of particles depending on the angle from which it is viewed. Dispense with formulæ to express a scientific generalisation and only analogy remains. Which of us outsiders has not often longed to hear from the physicist whether he is to take those representations with which the physicist tries to explain the world of atoms, as symbols or as the direct description of actual realities?

Science seems to have approached the very limits of our power of thought. It is a well-known fact that more than one physicist suffers this continuous working in a mental atmosphere for which the human organism does not seem to be adapted, as a heavy burden, oppressing him sometimes to the point of despair. Yet, desist he will not and cannot. The layman may indulge in a longing for the comfortably tangible reality of older days and reach for his Buffon to delight in that simple and serene representation of the world in which there is the scent of new-mown hay and the song of a lingering bird. But the science of yesterday has now become poetry and history.

I once asked De Sitter whether this longing for visions of yore ever broke through his thoughts of the expansion, the emptiness, or the spherical shape of the universe. The seriousness of his denial at once showed me the foolishness of my question.

Is the vertigo of our thinking at the infiniteness of knowledge perhaps similar to that which the mind had to conquer to dare the jump from the Ptolemaic to the Copernican view of the universe?

The categories with which thinking has contented itself so far seem to be in dissolution. Limits are effaced, contradictions appear compatible. Interdependence becomes the watchword of all modern observation of human and social processes. In sociology, economics, psychology or history, everywhere explanation in terms of direct orthodox cause and effect has had to make way for the recognition of many-sided composite relationships and mutual dependence. The concept of condition is supplanting that of cause.

One can go even further. Historic thinking is becoming increasingly antinomic and ambivalent. Antinomic: that this, the mind finds itself as it were suspended between two opposites which before seemed to exclude one another. Ambivalent: that is, our judgment, conscious of the relative merits of two opposing decisions, hesitates before the choice like the ass of Buridan.

Indeed, there is sufficient reason to speak of a crisis of modern thought and knowledge so violent and so far-reaching as can hardly be found in any known period of the past.

This intellectual side of the present cultural crisis has been taken as a starting-point partly because it can be ascertained and described with a much greater degree of objectivity than the disorders of social life, and because it allows of unbiased judgment. It lies outside the sphere of hostility, conflict and malevolence, at least most of it does. There is crisis but, strictly speaking, not illness or dislocation. It goes without saying that the term "intellectual crisis" must not be taken to refer to the struggles of politically controlled thinking, but to the progress of knowledge as such, as it manifests itself where the spirit still enjoys the freedom which it requires to be spirit. Apart from the strange concoctions like Marxian or Nordic mathematics which some in all seriousness would have us accept, this freedom has remained most inviolate in the field of the natural sciences and their guide, mathematics. There no prejudices disturb the progress of research. Natural science so far is international. The walling-in of nations has as yet done little harm to the international collaboration and communication of those engaged in the natural sciences. The subject practising them is still the human being without further qualification. The pursuit of the social sciences has of old been marked by a greater degree of susceptibility to the influence of national frontiers and national character. Due to the nature of its object, the study of human society has greater difficulty in raising itself to the degree of spiritual freedom which elevates it to the status of science. Nevertheless, the view to the horizon of the social sciences and the humanities is for the time being still relatively clear. What is really new in this field—significant change of method and insight, progressive enrichment and digestion of material, new synthesis—is not the work of the noisy satellites of a political system.

If scientific thought over the entire range finds itself in a state of crisis, therefore, it is a crisis from within and not one caused by contamination with the ills of a disordered society. Its roots lie in the mind's progress itself, leading science over almost inaccessible heights to summits where the path seems to lose itself. In the crisis of pure thought human folly or spiritual decay plays no part. It is the refinement of the means of understanding and the intensification of the will to knowledge itself which lie at the bottom of the ailment.

This crisis, then, is not only unavoidable but desirable and beneficial. On this point at least it is still always clear what our culture is striving for; it is pushing on with all the resources of increasing equipment, pushing on *through* the uncertainties and the insolvables of the present. The mind clearly sees the road which it must follow. There can be no stopping and no turning back.

The ascertainment of this simple fact that at least in one highly important field the course is inalterably set, should afford comfort and strength to those who would despair of the future of our culture. The crisis of scientific thinking may be bewildering in the highest degree; a reason for despondency it will be only to those who have not the courage to accept this world and this life as they have been given to us.

VII

WEAKENING OF JUDGMENT

When one turns from the creation of thought and knowledge to the manner in which knowledge is spread and thought is taken up and used, the aspect changes. The state of what may be called popular thinking is not only one of crisis but of a crisis full of decay and danger.

How naïve the glad and confident hope of a century ago, that the advance of science and the general extension of education assured the progressive perfection of society, seems to us to-day! Who can still seriously believe that the translation of scientific triumphs into still more marvellous technical achievements is enough to save civilization, or that the eradication of illiteracy means the end of barbarism! Modern society, with its intensive development and mechanisation, indeed looks very different from the dream vision of Progress!

The social life of our time shows a multitude of disquieting symptoms which can best be grouped under the heading "Weakening of Judgment." It is really rather disheartening. We live in a world which is infinitely better informed about itself, its nature and its possibilities than at any time in history. We know better than our ancestors what the universe is and how it functions, how the living organism operates, how the things of the spirit are related, how the historical sequence of events is to be understood. The human subject has more knowledge of himself and his world than ever before. Man has become greatly more capable of judgment, intensively in so far as the mind penetrates deeper into the composition and nature of things, extensively in so far as his knowledge extends over a very much wider range and especially in so far as a certain degree of knowledge is spread over a much greater number of individuals. Society regarded in the abstract knows itself. To "know thyself" was ever thought the essence

of wisdom. The conclusion would seem inescapable:
the world has grown wiser. *Risum teneatis.*

We know better. Folly in all its various forms, from
the frivolous and ridiculous to the wicked and destructive, was never so manifest throughout the world.
It is now no longer a theme for a clever and smiling
dissertation of a high-minded and gravely concerned
humanist like Erasmus. We must regard the infinite
folly of our time as a disease of society, analyse its
symptoms, and attempt soberly and realistically to
determine its nature with a view to seeking the means
of curing it.

The fallacy of the syllogism: "Self-knowledge is
wisdom—the world knows itself better than before—
ergo the world has grown wiser," originates with the
ambiguity of the terms. "The world" in the abstract
has neither knowledge nor power of action; it manifests itself solely through the thinking and action
of individuals. The term "knowledge," furthermore,
is anything but interchangeable with wisdom, a point
which hardly needs elaboration.

In a society characterised by universal popular education, extensive and immediate publicity of the day-
to-day life, and advanced division of labour, the

71

average person grows less and less dependent on his own faculties of thought and expression. On the surface this might seem paradoxical. For it is usually assumed that in a cultural environment of lesser intellectual intensity and with a relatively smaller spread of knowledge, individual thought will be under greater limitations, confined as it is within a narrow range of contacts, than in a more highly developed society. One associates with this more restricted thinking the qualities of conformity to pattern and sameness. This should not blind us to the fact, however, that with its more limited equipment and within this narrower range, such thinking centred on the subject's own sphere of life achieves a degree of independence which is lost in more intensively organised periods. The peasant, the mariner or the artisan of earlier times had in the sum total of his knowledge the pattern in which to view the world and its life. He knew himself unqualified to judge what lay beyond his ken (unless he were one of the professional talkers common to all times). He accepted authority knowing his judgment to be defective. In his acknowledged limitations lay his wisdom. It was the very limitation of his power of expression which, leaning on the pillars of the Holy Book and proverbial lore, often gave him style and eloquence.*

The modern organisation of knowledge-distribution is only too destructive of the beneficial effects of such intellectual limitations. To-day the average inhabitant of the western hemisphere knows a little of everything. He has the newspaper on his breakfast table and the wireless within reach. For the evening there is the film, cards, or a meeting to complete a day spent in the office or factory where nothing that is essential has been learnt. With slight variations this picture of a low cultural average holds good over the entire range, from factory-hand or clerk to manager or director. Only the personal will to culture, in whatever field and however pursued, raises modern man above this level. Observe that we speak here only of culture in the narrower sense of the possession of a certain treasure of beauty and wisdom. It is not impossible that the average person of limited culture nevertheless succeeds in raising his life to a higher

* During the Boer War participants and observers from the Netherlands were impressed with the ease of speech with which every Boer knew how to address those under his command.

level through his activity in other fields such as the religious or the social.

Even where there is a genuine desire for knowledge and beauty, the noisy obtrusiveness of the modern cultural apparatus still makes it very difficult for the average man to escape the danger of having his notions and values forced upon him. A knowledge which is as diversified as it is superficial and an intellectual horizon which is too wide for an eye unarmed with critical equipment, must inevitably lead to a weakening of the power of judgment.

This forcible feeding and defenceless acceptance of notions and values are not peculiar to the things of the intellect alone. In his appreciation of beauty and sentiments also the modern man labours under the strong pressure of low-quality mass-production. An excessive offer of trivial illusions supplies him with a hollow and false pattern for his tastes and feelings.

In this connection one other alarming but inescapable fact obtrudes. In older and more restricted forms of society man made his own entertainment. People sang, danced or played together. In the civilization of to-day all this has largely made way for watching others sing, dance or play. Of course there have always been performers and audiences. But the significant thing is that in our time the passive element is constantly gaining on the active one. Even in the field of sport, that vastly important part of modern culture, there is a growing tendency for the masses to have others play *for* them. This withdrawal from active participation in cultural activities has been rendered even more complete through the film and the radio. The transition from theatre to cinema is the transition from watching a play to watching the reflection of a play. Word and gesture are reduced from living action to mere reproduction. The voice carried through the ether is no more than an echo. Even the spectacle of sporting events comes to be replaced by the surrogates of ringside broadcasts and newspaper reports. All this contains an element of cultural enfeeblement and devitalisation. It is particularly apparent in one other important aspect of the cinematic art of to-day. Dramatic action itself is practically entirely expressed in the outwardly visible while the spoken word is relegated to a place of only secondary importance. The art of watching has become mere skill at rapid apperception and understanding of con-

75

tinuously changing visual images. The younger generation has acquired this cinematic perception to an amazing degree. This novel bent of mind, however, means the atrophy of a whole series of intellectual functions. To realise this one need only consider the difference between following a comedy of Molière and a film. Without claiming superiority of intellectual over visual understanding, one is nevertheless bound to admit that the cinema allows a number of æsthetic-intellectual means of perception to remain unexercised which cannot but lead to a weakening of judgment.

The mechanism of modern mass-entertainment, furthermore, is inimical to concentration. Mechanical reproduction of sound and spectacle virtually precludes the element of surrender and absorption: there is no awe, no stillness, no communing with the innermost self. Such stillness and communion with the soul, however, are the very things without which there can be no true culture.

The susceptibility of the average modern to pictorial suggestion enables advertising to exploit his lessened power of judgment. We are thinking here of both commercial advertising and political propaganda. Through an arresting picture the advertisement evokes the thought of gratifying a desire. The picture and the phrase are filled with as much sentiment as possible. They serve to create a mood disposing the mind towards formation of judgment at a passing glance. It is not easy to say how the advertisement works through in the individual brain and how it achieves its aim. Does the individual's decision to buy spring directly from his seeing or reading the advertisement? Or does the latter merely plant a memory in the consciousness of the multitude to which it reacts mechanically? Is there reason to speak of a certain intoxicating effect?—The operation of political propaganda is even more difficult to analyse. Has anyone on his way to the polls ever been moved in favour of a certain choice by the sight of the various swords, hatchets, hammers, cog-wheels, clenched fists, rising suns, bleeding hands and severe countenances which the political parties flourish before his eyes? We shall not try to answer the question. At any rate it is certain that the advertisement in all its forms speculates upon an enfeebled judgment and that through its inordinate extension the advertisement it-self contributes to this enfeeblement.

．　　　．　　　．

Our time, then, is faced by the discouraging fact that two highly vaunted achievements of civilization, universal education and modern publicity, instead of raising the level of culture, appear ultimately to produce certain symptoms of cultural devitalisation and degeneration. The masses are fed with an hitherto undreamt-of quantity of knowledge of all sorts, but there is something wrong with its assimilation. Un-digested knowledge hampers judgment and stands in the way of wisdom.

Has society no way of escape from this process of intellectual and spiritual cheapening? Is it to go on ever further? Or will it reach a point of all-pervading extension where it will work itself out? These are questions which must wait till we formulate the con-clusions of this study and which, even then, will find no definite answer. For the moment there are other signs of cultural degeneration which must first be considered.

VIII

THE DECLINE OF THE CRITICAL SPIRIT

Apart from the general weakening of judgment which we discussed in the foregoing, there is reason to speak also of a weakening of the critical spirit, a decline of the critical capacities, a diminishing regard for truth, this time not as a mass phenomenon of the consumers of knowledge but as an organic failing on the part of those who produce it. Related to this decadence-symptom there is still another which we may call the perversion of the function of science or the misuse of science as a means. Let us attempt to deal with this group of phenomena.

At the same moment that science began to reveal its formerly undreamt-of potentialities for dominating nature, vastly extending human power by virtue of its new depth of insight, its capacity to serve as a touchstone of pure knowledge and a guide rule for life declined. The proportion between its various functions changed.

These functions have long been threefold: acquisition and extension of knowledge, education of society to higher and purer forms of civilization, and creation of means to adapt and control natural forces. During the rise of modern science in the seventeenth and eighteenth centuries the first two functions generally kept pace with one another while the third still lagged far behind. The advance of knowledge and the recession of ignorance and superstition filled people with enthusiasm. There was not a soul to doubt the high educational and guidance value of science at that time. More was built on it than its foundations could ever support. With every new discovery the world and its processes came to be better understood. A certain ethical gain was implied in this growing lucidity of the enquiring mind. Meanwhile, what we have called the third function of science, the creation of technical means, made relatively little progress. Electricity was a curiosity for the educated public. Up till the beginning of the nineteenth century the age-old forms of traction and transmission of power remained virtually unchallenged. For the eighteenth century one might express the relationship between the three functions of science, extension of knowledge, education, and creation of technical means, in the series 8 : 4 : 1.

If one desired to give numerical expression to their relationship in our time it might be 2 : 16 : 16, for instance. The proportion between the three functions has become an entirely different one. Perhaps this low estimate of the educational value of science relative to its knowledge and application values will arouse a storm of protest. And yet, could anyone maintain that the marvellous discoveries of modern science, inaccessible to the minds of any but the initiated few, as they necessarily must be, still continue to contribute materially to the general level of culture? Even the best teaching at universities and inferior educational institutions cannot alter the fact that, while the acquisition of knowledge and its technical application are still daily progressing at an astounding pace, the educational value of science is now no greater than it was a century ago.

The human being of to-day seldom, if ever, looks

to science * for his philosophy of life. It is not science itself which is to blame. There is a strong tendency away from science. People no longer believe in its capacity for guidance, and not altogether without reason; there has been a time when science claimed too large a share of the world's mastery. But there is also something else besides natural reaction: deterioration of the intellectual conscience. The impulse to achieve a maximum of objectivity and exactness in thinking on the rationally comprehensible, and to apply the test of criticism to such thinking, is weakening. A vast and murky twilight seems to have spread over numberless minds. All the delimitations between the logical, the æsthetic and the emotive functions are purposely ignored. Sentiment is allowed to play a part in forming judgment regardless of the object of judgment and in direct negation of the claims of the critical intellect. Intuition is called upon to justify a choice which in reality is based on emotional predisposition. Interest and desire are confused with consciousness of truth. And to justify all this, what

* Translator's Note: The word "science" is used throughout in its wider meaning of the pursuit of knowledge in general— the German *Wissenschaft*.

actually is the abandonment of the logical principle itself is paraded as the necessary revolt against the supreme rule of reason.

We have all long since outgrown the belief in a tyrannically consistent rationalism. We realise that not everything can be measured by reason. The advance of thought itself has brought us this realisation. A richer and deeper understanding than the solely rational has given greater meaning to our knowledge. But where the wise man, through freer and ampler judgment, finds a deeper sense in things and life, the fool finds in this freedom only licence for greater nonsense. It is a truly tragic consequence: in the process of realising the limitations of reason the modern mind has become susceptible to absurdities to which it had long been immune.

The neglect of the veto of criticism can best be illustrated with a few words about racial theories. Anthropology is an important branch of natural history. It is a biological science with a strong historical element like geology and palæontology. Through exact methodical research based on principles of heredity, it has constructed a system of race differentiation whose utility yields only to that of other biological constructions, inasmuch as the criterion of skull measurement on which its conclusions are based leaves a relatively wide margin of doubt. The physical characteristics by which anthropology with varying degrees of positivity distinguishes races seem in general to be correlated with certain intellectual and spiritual features. The Chinese differ from the English not only in appearance but in spirit also. To make this statement, however, means that in the consideration of the phenomenon of race one has unwittingly included that of culture. For the Chinese and the English are products of race plus culture. In other words, the ascertainment of intellectual and spiritual race qualities is only possible after adding to the object under investigation (race) the anthropologically immeasurable element of culture. To assume an exclusively biological determination of spiritual race qualities is an obvious fallacy. For it is incontestable that at least some of the spiritual features of a race owe their development to the conditions and environment in which the particular race has grown up. A scientific separation of this extraneous element from the supposedly indigenous one is not possible. Nor can any research establish specific

84

correlations connecting the physical peculiarities of a race with their intellectual counterparts (assuming that such intellectual characteristics could be shown to be common to an entire race at all). As long as anthropology suffers from these inabilities the belief that character is determined by race must continue to lack scientific support. Even when surrounded with the necessary reservations it remains uncertain and indefinite knowledge. But if one accepts the reservation that the concept of race cannot be handled without qualifying it with that of culture, one thereby virtually abandons the claim to a scientifically formulated principle of race, in which case one will do well not to build any conclusions on it.

For instance, if intellectual genius could be traced to race, then it would seem evident that, conversely, similarity of race ought to follow from similarity of genius. The Jews and the Germans have a striking genius for philosophy and music. Conclusion: there must be a strong racial affinity between the Germans and the Jews. The conclusion is absurd, but no more absurd than those which nowadays enjoy popularity with vast numbers of educated people.

The current vogue for racial theories in their political and cultural application is not due to any particular obtrusion of the science of anthropology. It is rather an instance of the vindication of a popular doctrine which for a long time and until recently had never been able to pass the tests necessary to gain admittance to the domain of critically verified knowledge. From the outset rejected as untenable by genuine science, the doctrine of racial superiority had carried on its existence for half a century in a sphere of romantic fancy and sham erudition until political circumstances suddenly placed it on a pedestal from which it now dares to dictate scientific truths. This doctrine of superiority based on alleged racial purity has always exercised a strong attraction for the popular mind, because it is essentially cheap and because it appeals to a romantic spirit uncontrolled by the critical impulse and preoccupied with a desire for self-glorification. It was the fumes of a stale romanticism which clouded the spirits of men like H. S. Chamberlain, Schemann and Woltmann. The success of the views propounded by Madison Grant and Lothrop Stoddard, who branded the labourer as belonging to an inferior race, was of a malodorous political flavour.

86

The argument of race in cultural conflicts is always self-praise. Has a race-theorist ever made the startling and shaming discovery that the race to which he deemed himself to belong is inferior? The motive is always exaltation of self and kin over others and at the expense of others. The racial thesis is always hostile, always *anti,* a bad sign for a doctrine which claims to be scientific. The racially inspired attitude is anti-Asiatic, anti-African, anti-proletarian, anti-Semitic.

It must be clearly understood that we are not denying the existence of serious problems and conflicts of a social, economic, or political nature arising from the contiguity of two races within one state or region. Nor do we deny that the feelings of one race for another may be in the nature of instinctive aversion. In both cases, however, the dividing element is irrational and it is not the task of science to present this irrational moment as a critically established rule of conduct. The existence of these racial aversions renders the quasi-scientific nature of applied theories of race all the more evident.

If an instinctive racial aversion is indeed biologically determined (as would seem to be the case with those to whom the odour of the negro is decidedly offensive), the civilized person of only a short time ago would have considered it his duty to render himself account of the animal quality of this reaction and to control it as much as possible instead of fostering it and priding himself on it. A society built on Christian foundations has never had room for a policy planned on "a zoological basis," as the Ósservatore Romano so aptly called it. In a society which leaves free play to racial hostility and even encourages it, the condition "culture is control over nature" remains unfulfilled.

In the condemnation of politically applied race theories one must make two reservations. First, there must be no confusion with a well-considered policy of practical eugenics. What the latter may still do for the public weal need not be considered here. Secondly, the self-exaltation of one people over another need not necessarily be rooted in racial pretensions. The Latin peoples' feeling of superiority has always been based on cultural qualities rather than on race. The French *la race* has never acquired that pure anthropological ring. Pride and self-exaltation in cultural nobility may sometimes be slightly more rational and even somewhat more legitimate than racial pride; they are forms of intellectual vanity none the less.

From whichever angle one looks at it, the application of racial theories remains a striking proof of the lowered demands of public opinion upon the purity of critical judgment. The brakes of criticism are slipping.

The brakes are failing in other respects as well. It is undeniable that with the renewed desire for synthesis in the social sciences, in itself a healthy and beneficial reaction against the excessive analysis of a preceding period, the "hunch" has come to play a growing part in scientific production. There is an unending succession of bold syntheses, often constructed with great skill and erudition, in which the "originality" of the author enjoys greater triumphs than would seem compatible with sober-minded science. The social philosopher sometimes assumes the rôle of the *bel esprit* of former ages, but it is often not quite clear whether in so doing he takes himself seriously, though he certainly intends to be taken seriously by his readers. The result is something which stands in between cultural philosophy and cultural fantasy. A strong tendency towards æsthetic forms of expression often adds still more to the confused character of the product.

The natural sciences are not plagued with afflictions of this type. They have in the mathematical formula the immediate test of the veracity, not of the validity, of their products. In their domain there is no place for the *bel esprit* and the charlatan is immediately expelled. It is both the privilege and the danger of the humanities that for expressing their ideas they need notions lying beyond the sphere of pure reason in the domain of æsthetic perception.

Over the entire range of the non-exact sciences judgment has become less definite, in contrast with the natural sciences which are able to demand ever greater accuracy of statement. The thoroughly rational is no longer the unchallenged instrument it used to be. Judgment is less tempered by formula and tradition than before. How popular and indispensable have words like "vision," "conception" or "introspection" become to indicate the process of forming knowledge! All this has brought a large measure of indefiniteness to judgment. This indefiniteness *may* be beneficial. But it carries with it the danger of intellectual vacillation between steady conviction and an easy toying with ideas. In view of the antinomic quality of thinking in general, already commented upon, the decision: "This I really think" has become greatly more difficult for the rigorously self-critical mind. For the shallow or prejudiced mind it has become all the more easy.

The lowering of the standards of critical judgment has, I think, been promoted in no small degree by the trend of thought which may be called the Freudian. Freudian psychiatry discovered significant data whose interpretation led research from the field of psychology on to that of sociology and culture. Then the not unusual phenomenon occurred that the mind trained in exact observation and analysis, when faced with the task of sociological, that is, inexact interpretation, shows itself completely lacking in norms by which to judge and evaluate scientific evidence. And thus in this unfamiliar field it is led to jump from any "hunch" to the most far-reaching conclusions which would crumble into nothingness the moment they were subjected to the test of the philosophical-historical method. If, then, the constructions so arrived at are furthermore accepted in wide circles as recognised truths, and their technical terms passed about as ready-made instruments of thought, large groups of a low critical average are accordingly given a welcome opportunity to play at science to their hearts' content. Think only of the pitiful exhibitions of the authors of popular dissertations who explain everything about man and his world in psycho-analytical terms, building their spacious theories and conclusions on "symbols," "complexes" and "phases of infantile psychic life"!

IX

SCIENCE MISUSED

The theories of race showed us an example of quasi-science usurping the place of true science in order to serve Might. In true science, directed towards the devising and construction of means of power, Might finds a still stronger instrument for the furtherance of its ends. "Knowledge is Power," once the jubilant cry of the Victorian era, has now begun to have a sinister ring in our ears.

Science, unguided by a higher abstract principle, freely hands over its secrets to a vastly developed and commercially inspired technology, and the latter, even less restrained by a supreme culture saving principle, with the means of science creates all the instruments of power demanded from it by the organisation of

Might. Technology produces all that society requires for the perfection of communication and the gratification of wants. Its possibilities are still far from exhausted. Each fresh scientific discovery opens new prospects, but in its present structure society is not yet capable of assimilating all the innovations and improvements which technology has to offer in the way of living accommodation, nutrition, communication and transmission of thought.

Society demands from applied science means of destruction as well. Destruction of life is not always warfare and crime. To combat the plagues with which the vegetable and animal worlds threaten the human race must be deemed permissible and even obligatory by every community which does not, like some Indian religions, subscribe to the extreme view of absolute non-resistance. Maintenance of order and enforcement of law may require force, even to the point of destruction of human life.

One step further brings us to the use of science to smother the germ of life. Prevention of conception through artificial means *may* promote social welfare and happiness. The term "control over nature" which we deemed essential for culture is not quite applicable here. It is not control over nature but frustration of nature, potential destruction. The point where the use of science to this end becomes misuse depends on the ethical attitude towards birth control which, again, is to a large extent governed by the religious point of view.

Apart altogether from the ethical delineation between use and misuse in this respect, there is the question of the social consequences of consistent birth control. To many it augurs progressive racial extinction with the inevitable concomitant of cultural destruction. According to calculations based on demography, a continuance of the present rate of decline of the birth-rate of most Western European countries would suffice to assure the disappearance of the native populations within a few generations. If this be true, the problem of the crisis of civilization loses much of its urgency, for in that case its negative outcome would be certain from the outset. Why attempt to safeguard a civilization if the heirs to which it is to pass are lacking?

Be this as it may, the fact that science has made birth control technically possible and hygienically harmless cannot unconditionally entitle it to the claim of having fulfilled its function of promoting the common weal and raising the level of culture in this respect.

The question of use or misuse of science grows far more acute when one looks to the production of means for the direct, large-scale destruction of human life and property. The writer of these pages is neither a radical pacifist nor a believer in absolute non-resistance. Not only does his condemnation of killing stop at individual self-defence and safe-guarding of law and order, but also he holds the view that the citizen has to serve his country, to kill and to die, when his military duty commands. He is of the opinion, however, that it is possible to conceive of certain circumstances under which the self-willed extinction of an entire generation would be preferable to the survival of some through the guilt of all.

The World War through which we have passed has stretched our conceptions of the politically permissible to the breaking-point. We have understood and we have suffered that, given the fact of war, the perfection of scientific technology could hardly permit the new means of destruction of a chemical and ballistic nature, in the air and under water, to remain unused. We see with a feeling of helpless revolt how scientific technology all the world over continues to manufacture and to perfect these weapons. But there is a point where our personal willingness to accept all this ought to break down: that is bacterial warfare. The fact seems to have been established beyond reasonable doubt that the possibilities of waging war through the dissemination of disease germs, openly advocated by some, are being seriously studied and furthered in more than one country.* Now it may be asked: what is the difference between operating with explosives, gas or bacteria? Did not the combatants of earlier times poison springs?—Indeed, the difference is merely one of sentiment. But if it has come to this, that men *with the help of science* are to fight each other with what all earlier civilizations, from the lowest to the highest, have bowed to as the work of God, Fate, Demon or Nature, this will be such a Satanic blasphemy against the Principle of this world that it will be better for a culpable humanity to perish in its own iniquity.

* *Cf.* P. A. Gorer's contribution *Bacterial Warfare* to the collection of papers, The Frustration of Science, New York: W. W. Norton & Company, Inc.

Even if this civilization in which we live is to recover its material and moral health, the fact alone that bacterial warfare has been seriously considered will remain an everlasting and terrible stigma on an unworthy generation.

X

THE DISAVOWAL OF THE INTELLECTUAL PRINCIPLE

Decline of the critical spirit, weakening of judgment, perversion of the function of science, all point to a serious cultural disorder. To think, however, that in locating these symptoms one is attacking the evil at its roots, is to make a grave mistake. For already we hear the swelling chorus of objections from the self-styled bearers of a new culture: "But we do not want a tried and tested knowledge to rule us and to decide over our actions; our aim is not to think and to know but to live and to do."

Here we have the pivotal point of the present crisis of civilization: the conflict between *knowing* and *being,* between intelligence and existence. There is

99

nothing novel about it. The essential insufficiency of
our understanding was already realised in the earliest
days of philosophy. The reality in and through which
we live is in its essence unknowable, inaccessible to
the processes of the mind, absolutely disparate from
thought. In the first half of the nineteenth century
this old truth, already understood by a Nicolaus
Cusanus, is taken up again by Kierkegaard, whose
philosophy centres upon the antithesis of existing and
thinking. It served him to found his faith all the more
firmly. It was not until much later that other thinkers
forced this thought on to tracks away from God and
let it derail in nihilism and despair, or in worship
of earthly life. Nietzsche, deeply convinced of man's
tragic exile from truth and interpreting the will to
life as will to power, repudiated the intellectual principle with all the poetical vigour of his genius. Prag-
matism deprived the concept truth of its claim to
absolute validity by placing it in the flow of time.
To the pragmatists truth is what has essential validity
for those professing it. Something is true when and
in so far as it is valid for a particular time. A crude
mind could easily think: something is valid, there-

fore it is true. A truth-concept reduced to only relative value was bound to bring a kind of ideological egalitarianism, an abolition of all differences of rank and value of ideas, in its wake. Sociological thinkers like Max Weber, Max Scheler, Karl Mannheim and Oswald Spengler have of late introduced the term of the *Seinsverbundenheit des Denkens,* which may be very imperfectly rendered with "the environment- or life-conditioned nature of thought." The concept itself makes them next-door neighbours to historical materialism, which is professedly anti-intellectual. Thus the tendencies of a whole age which, to avoid the vagueness of "anti-intellectual," we venture to call anti-noetic, merged into a mighty stream which shortly was to threaten what were long thought to be insurmountable barriers of intellectual culture. It was Georges Sorel who, in his *Réflexions sur la Violence,* formulated the practical political consequences of all this, thereby becoming the spiritual father of all modern dictatorships.

But it is not only the dictators and their followers who desire the subjugation of the will to knowledge to the vital impulse. We have here the most fundamental element of the cultural crisis as a whole. This revulsion of the spirit is the essential process dominating the situation in which we find ourselves to-day.

Was it philosophical thought which led the way and society which followed? Or do we have to reverse the order and admit that it is a case of thought dancing to the tune of life? The doctrine itself which subjugates knowledge to life seems to impose the latter view.

Have earlier generations ever renounced the intellectual principle in this way? It seems impossible to find historical parallels. Systematic philosophical and practical anti-intellectualism such as we are witnessing, appears to be something truly novel in the history of human culture. To be sure, the past has often known reactions of thought whereby a too exclusive primacy of the understanding was succeeded by a revindication of the will. This is what happened, for instance, when the thought of Duns Scotus took its place beside that of Thomas Aquinas. These spiritual reactions, however, were not concerned with practical life or the worldly order but with the Faith, the striving for the ultimate meaning of life. And this striving itself always remained an "apprehending," however far reason was left behind. The modern mind too often confuses intellectualism with rationalism. Even those forms of approach which, transgressing the purely intellectual, were intended to attain through insight and contemplation what was inaccessible to the understanding, always remained directed towards knowledge of truth. The Greek or the Indian word for it, *gnosis* or *jnâna,* makes it clear enough that even the purest mysticism remains a "knowing." It is always the spirit which moves in the world of the intelligible. To have truth was always the ideal. There are no instances known to me of cultures having forsaken Truth or renounced the understanding in its widest sense.

When earlier currents of thought repudiated allegiance to Reason it was always in favour of the super-rational. What parades as the culture of to-day does not only disavow Reason but also the knowable itself, and this in favour of the sub-rational, the passions and the instincts. It votes for the will, not in the sense of Duns Scotus, however, but for the will to worldly power, for "existence," for "blood and soil," instead of "understanding" and "spirit." *

* For the answer to the question how Hegel's dictum is to be understood that philosophy is *"Ihre Zeit in Gedanken erfasst,"* see Th. Litt, *Philosophie und Zeitgeist,* where the complete lack of justification with which those professing the *Lebensphilosophie* claim themselves the disciples of Hegel in this respect is clearly demonstrated.

XI

THE WORSHIP OF LIFE

THE next addition to the collection of intellectually fashionable words will doubtless be "existential." I can see it springing up on all sides. Before long it will have landed with the public at large. When, in order to convince one's audience of profundity, one has said "dynamic" long enough, it will be "existential." The word will serve to forsake the spirit all the more solemnly, a sneer at all that is knowledge and truth.

At meetings of scholars statements are heard which even a short time ago would have been thought too senseless to be comical. According to newspaper reports, a speaker at the Congress of Philologists held in Treves in October, 1934, declared that what one should expect from science was not so much truth as "whetted swords." When another of those present showed himself lacking in respect for certain instances of nationalist interpretation of history, he was reproached by the chairman with "lack of subjectivity." Note, all this at a congress of scholars.

This is what our civilized world has come to. Let it not be thought that the degeneration of the critical spirit confines itself to the countries where extreme nationalism has triumphed. Any observer can find numerous proofs in his own environment of a certain indifference of large numbers of educated people to the degree of truth embodied in the figures of their world of ideas. The categories fiction and history, in their simple and current meaning, are no longer clearly distinguished. It is no longer asked whether the truth-content of intellectual matter is up to standard. The ascendancy of the concept "mythos" is the clearest example. People accept a representation in which the elements of wish and fantasy are purposely included but which nevertheless proclaims to represent "the past" and to serve as a guide-rule for life, thereby hopelessly confusing the spheres of knowledge and will.

"Existence-conditioned" thought striving for expression allows fanciful allegory to creep into logical argument, unchecked by critical reasoning. If life cannot be expressed in terms of logic, as everyone must admit to be the case, then it is for the poet to step in where the logical approach fails. Thus it has been as long as the world has known the art of poetry. In the process of cultural development, however, thinker and poet came to be clearly distinguished, and each was allotted his own domain. Of late the new "life philosophy" has shown a tendency to relapse into a bewildering confusion of logical and poetical means of expression. Among the latter the blood-metaphor occupies an especially prominent place. The poets and the sages of all peoples and ages have always made a ready use of the image of "the blood" to catch an active principle of life in one striking word. Although, abstractly speaking, other humours would have been just as capable of conveying the suggestion of heredity and relationship, in blood one saw, felt, and heard the flow of life; in the shedding of blood one saw life ebbing away; blood stood for courage and battle. The image of blood has of old had a sacred content also; in fact, it became the expression of the most profound divine mystery while at the same time it remained a meaningful term for the most prosaic proverb. While it should be no cause for surprise, therefore, that this old image of the blood should still enjoy widespread popularity one may, nevertheless, well feel wonder to see it now restored to the rank of an official term in the juridical phraseology of a great modern nation.

The order of precedence of blood and spirit has been completely reversed by the apostles of the life philosophy. Of the philosopher R. Müller-Freienfels I find quoted: "The essence of our mind lies not in purely intellectual understanding, but in its biological function as a means for the preservation of life." Let no one dare to attribute this function to "the blood"!

The obsession with life is to be viewed as a manifestation of excessive full-bloodedness, to remain in the terminology of the life-philosophy. Through the technical perfection of all comforts of life, the in every way increased security of life, the greater accessibility of all types of pleasure, and the vast and still lingering growth of material prosperity, society has got into a state which in the old pathology might have been called a "plethora." We have been living in spiritual and material superabundance. We are so preoccupied with life because it is made so easy for us. The ever-growing power of observation and the facility of intellectual communication have made life strong and bold. Till well into the middle of the nineteenth century even the well-to-do section of European society was in much more direct and constant contact with the miseries of existence than we are to-day and think our due. Our own grandfathers were given only very limited possibilities of killing pain, healing wounds or fractures, shutting out cold, expelling darkness, communicating with others directly or indirectly, avoiding filth and stench. On all sides man was continually made to feel the natural limitations of earthly well-being. The efficient ministering of the technical, hygienic and sanitary appliances with which man has surrounded himself is spoiling him. He is losing the good-humoured resignation in the daily imperfections of human well-being which formed the discipline of earlier generations. But at the same time he runs the risk of losing the natural ability to take human happiness as it offers itself, as well. Life is made too easy. Mankind's moral fibre is giving way under the softening in-fluence of luxury.

In earlier civilizations, whether Christian, Moslem, Buddhist or any other, there was always this contrast: in principle the value of earthly happiness is depre-cated relatively to celestial bliss or union with the All. As all these religions, however, do recognise a relative worth of earthly pleasures, and consider them as God-given, denial of the value of life meant in-gratitude. It was the very realisation of the precarious-ness of every moment of human well-being which caused it to be appreciated at its true value. A steady orientation on the hereafter may lead to a renuncia-tion of the terrestrial, but it does not permit of *Welt-schmerz*.

In the present there is a contrast also, but it is a very different one. The increase of security, of com-fort, and of the possibilities of want-gratification, in short the greater ease of living, has had two results. On the one hand, it has prepared the soil for all forms of renunciation of life: philosophical denial of its value, purely emotive spleen or aversion from life; on the other, it has instilled the belief in the right to happiness. It has made people expect things from life. Related to this there is another contrast. The ambivalent attitude which wavers between the renunciation and the enjoyment of life is peculiar to the individual alone. The community, however, without hesitation and with more conviction than ever before, accepts earthly life as the object of all striving and action. It is indeed a true worship of life.

Now it is a question for serious consideration whether any advanced culture can survive without a certain measure of orientation on Death. The great civilizations of the past have all had it. There are signs that the philosophical thought of to-day is also coming to it. It seems only logical, moreover, that a philosophy which rates "living" above "knowing" should also include the end of life in its vision.

These are strange times. Reason, which once combated faith and seemed to have conquered it, now has to look to faith to save it from dissolution. For it is only on the unshaken and unyielding foundation of a living metaphysical belief that the concept of absolute truth, with its consequence of absolute validity of ethical norms, can withstand the growing pressure of the instinctive will to live.

Wondrous illusion! Knowledge and understanding are violently attacked from all sides, but always with the weapons of semi-knowledge and misunderstanding. To prove the inutility of the intellectual instrument one has no alternative but to appeal to other knowledge than that which is scorned. Reality and life itself remain inscrutable and mute. All speaking implies knowing. Even the poetry which most passionately attempts to penetrate to the core of life itself (I am thinking of Whitman and certain poems of Rilke) remains a product of the mind, a knowing. To take the anti-noetic principle seriously and consistently is to deny oneself the power of speech.

A philosophy which from the outset declares its basic truths to be conditioned by the particular organisation of life which it serves, is really superfluous for the upholders of this organisation and worthless for the rest of the world. It serves only to support and to rationalise the existing order. Why, if it is not knowledge and understanding that matter, why, then, enlist the thinkers in the service of the all-powerful State to prove its value? Give them a spade, a marital bed and a yard of gold braid.

XII

LIFE AND BATTLE

LIFE is battle. It is an ancient truth. Christianity has always known it. Its validity as an essential principle of culture is already implied in our premiss that all culture includes an element of striving. Striving is always battle—struggle, that is—the exercise of will and strength to overcome resistances which stand in the way of the attainment of an aim. Almost all action of the human soul is expressed in terms of combat. One of the most essential characteristics of the living organism is that it is more or less equipped for the attitude of battle. The identification of life and battle is just as adequate in the purely biological as in the spiritual sense. There will be few truths which a school of thought bent on subjugating everything to the claims of life will be more eager to preach. But what will be the meaning it attaches thereto?

The essence and the ideal of Christian thought implied the designation of evil as the object of combat. Evil was the negation of all that revelation proclaims and conscience avows as the manifestation of divine will, wisdom, and goodness. In ultimate instance this is the field where the battle can be waged *by* man *against* the evil *within* himself. As the knowledge of good and evil, truth and untruth, comes to be organised in Church, community or earthly domination, the battle against evil acquires an extensive form and outward direction as well. It became the Christian's duty to wage war on the wicked. The tragedy of earthly existence, the state of interlacement and intermixture of the *Civitas Dei* and the *Civitas Terrena,* has made the history of Christendom, meaning thereby the history of the Christian peoples, a very different thing from the triumph of Christianity. The authority at whose instance the wicked were designated has in turn been that of theological parties in the grip of dogmatic fervour, of uncivilized empires, of Churches fighting for their existence, of passionately believing and wildly covetous peoples, of governments entangled in Church conflicts. But whether one looks at the old councils, the Crusades, the struggle between emperor and pope, or the religious wars, the belief that the enmity was founded in the true recognition of good and evil, truth and untruth, always remained intact. This same conviction—or should we say presumption?—decided on the degree and the means of violence permitted to the Christian in his fight against the foes of true religion. Within the limits of Christian doctrine the needle of human conscience could indicate the Christian's duty along a scale which went from absolute non-resistance to ruthless warfare.

When the generally held convictions of to-day regarding good and evil are tested by the Christian principle or from even a platonic point of view, it appears that in theory the fundamentals of Christianity have been abandoned along a much larger front than that of its official or semi-official abjuration. The question to what extent this is true of the individual conscience will be dealt with at a later point. It is certain, however, that in current thinking on the duties of the community, the notion of absolute good and evil plays a relatively insignificant rôle. For large numbers the idea of life-struggle has been transferred from the domain of the individual conscience to that of the public life of the community. In this transfer the idea has lost much of its ethical content. The life-struggle which is accepted as fate and duty appears almost exclusively as the struggle of a certain community for a certain common weal, that is, as a cultural task. It is a struggle against certain public evils. In the condemnation of such evils there may be a sincere ethical element, as, for instance, with crime, prostitution or pauperism. But the more the particular evil threatens the community as such, as in the case of economic depression or political difficulties, the more the notion of evil is reduced to that of an internal weakness to be overcome or an external resistance to be defeated.

In view of the fact, however, that man by nature remains disposed to moral indignation and condemnation of others, even though intellectually he may have repudiated all ethical standards, this feeling of troublesome weakness or importunate resistance is still always tinged with a certain horror of evil or wickedness, and thus the confusion can easily arise where every resistance is viewed and felt as evil and wicked.

The resistances with which a community thinks itself threatened are usually exercised by other human groups. The life-struggle as a public duty then becomes a struggle of men against men. These *others* against whom the fight is directed theoretically no longer appear in the guise of "the wicked." In the struggle for power or wealth they are simply rivals, or political or economic oppressors. According to the particular position of the subject group, they are commercial competitors or those in possession of the means of production, the bearers of undesirable biological characteristics or simply related or unrelated neighbours, or, again, those who stand in the way of an expansion of might. In all these cases the will to combat, to subjugate, to expel, to expropriate or to extinguish is not founded in an ethical condemnation as such. But human nature remains weak, much as an heroic paganism may refuse to recognise such weakness. Thus into every struggle against resistances creeps Hatred, Hatred which only pure wickedness of the antagonists would partly justify.

Every psychological reaction to which the masses are subject casts its spell upon the community seeking battle or fearing it. Especially the dread of the unknown looming in the distance has a fateful effect. The more powerful the technical equipment and the more extensive and immediate human intercourse, the greater the danger that political tensions, despite the desire to avoid extremes, will relieve themselves in the precipitate and, in the long run, ineffectual form which we call war.

Honour be to the soldier in the field. In the acute agonies and miseries of war he recaptures all the highest values of *askesis*. He, for one, has no hate. In permanent and conscious readiness for unqualified self-sacrifice, in absolute subservience to a purpose in whose determination he has had no part, he discharges a task demanding the highest fulfilment of his ethical functions.

Can one proceed from this recognised impeccability of the soldier to the vindication of the impeccability of political hostility in general or, in other words, of the good right of a State to wage war for its own interests? The question is answered in the affirmative by a political theory which at present, especially in Germany, has found favour with great numbers of thinkers and men of action alike. With extremely simple reasoning it eliminates from inter-State relationships any and all elements of human malice.

To do this all that is necessary is to construct an *a priori* which places the State as an absolute independent object on a level of philosophical equivalence with the spiritual domain to which the concepts of truth and justice belong. This is what Carl Schmitt, with great ingenuity, has set out to do in his treatise, *Der Begriff des Politischen*.* The discussion opens with the following words: "The essential political distinction is that between Friend and Foe. It gives human actions and motives their political meaning. All political actions and motives can, in ultimate instance, be traced to this distinction. In so far as the opposition is not to be derived from other characteristics, it corresponds as a political concept to the relatively independent characteristics of other

---

* C. Schmitt, *Der Begriff des Politischen,* third edition. Hamburg (1933), Hanseatische Verlagsanstalt. The first edition dates from 1927.

contrasts: good and wicked in the ethical domain, beautiful and ugly in the æsthetic, useful and harmful in the economic; it is, at any rate, an absolute category . . ."

Now, it seems to me that in this construction of the political as an absolute category we have a case of an express and implicitly admitted *petitio principii*. The postulate which it would have us acknowledge, moreover, is one which no one whose philosophy of life still has the slightest contact with Plato (in spite of his glorification of the *politeia*), with Christianity or with Kant could accept.

If it were admissible that in general the opposition friend-foe were of the same category as the others mentioned above, it would indeed follow that in the political field for which this opposition is held to be decisive, the friend-foe opposition would override all other oppositions. The end of the first paragraph of Schmitt's discussion reads: "The absolute nature of the political immediately shows itself in the fact that it is possible to separate a specific opposition such as that of friend and foe from all other oppositions and to understand it as an entirely independent entity." Is not this over-rating the power of the logical argument as such, in a manner which is strongly reminiscent of the infancy of scholasticism? Is not the thinking of this shrewd jurist from the outset caught in the most vicious of vicious circles?

The writer has no difficulty in divesting the idea of Foe of its ethical associations by identifying it with πολέμιοσ, *hostis* (public enemy), and not with εχθρόσ, *inimicus* (private or personal enemy).* Very properly he points out that Mtth. 5, 44 en Luc. 6, 27, do not read: *diligite hostes vestros,* but: *inimicos.* Equally true is it that from the beginning the practice of Christianity has always known and recognised the concept of *hostes,* i.e., public enemies, and that the Gospel word quoted above has no bearing on the political domain, therefore. Whether this is sufficient justification for placing the political enmity relationship (it is clear that "friend" has, in reality, no positive meaning here) on the same level with true-false or good-evil, is another point altogether and one which, regardless of whether or not the Christian principle is accepted, can hardly be conceded.

It would seem more logical to replace the friend-foe opposition with that of weak-strong, for friend

* Pp. 10, 11.

means nothing in this opposition and *foe* simply means *opponent*. In the long run, however, there can be no permanent equality of opposing forces in any conflict. Thus it appears that this thesis implies the unqualified recognition of the principle: *Might is Right*.

Let us assume the author's point of view, however, and view its consequences. This point of view implies that the submission of political conflicts to the judgment of a third party is rejected as unreasonable, foolish and useless.* The State, and therefore in principle every State, is the one and only judge of *how* and *when* to combat the enemy † and—it would seem to follow—also of *who* is to be regarded as enemy. To the State finally, according to this reasoning, would fall the decision as to whether or not the subject of political action has the character of a State itself, that is, whether it has the right to have foes.

* P. 8.

† P. 28. The acclaim with which Schmitt's doctrine has been met is illustrated by its widespread application to the task of social science in general, in accordance with the tenets of the "Life-Philosophy." A certain W. Behne demands that "social science shall adapt and interpret its findings politically, that is, in accordance with the friend-foe relationship and with regard to the true existence of our nation." *Vergangenheit und Gegenwart*, 24, 1934, pp. 660–70.

This is a crux whose consequences the author has apparently not fully realised, or at least has failed to consider. Is a group which desires to become politically independent entitled to conduct itself politically? What of the members of a federation, what of a party or a class demanding the leadership of the State? The conclusion seems inescapable that in all such instances the determination of political character, that is the decision as to whether a group is entitled to conduct itself as a State, lies with the struggle-seeking group itself. In the shadow of the recognition of absolute independence of the political as such, therefore, stands the recognition of anarchism.

It is evident, moreover, that inasmuch as the State is held to be the sole judge of the desirability of extending its sphere of power, and as such extension in every case may be declared to be a condition of survival, the subjugation of the smaller by the larger States becomes simply a question of inclination and opportunity.

Next to the prophets of political totalitarianism stand the advocates of war for war's sake. Conquest is the State's fundamental condition of survival. This is the view of the well-known sociologist, Hans

Freyer: "To make itself felt as a State among others, the State (needs) a sphere of conquest around it. It must conquer to be." * More succinct denial of the small State's right to existence is well-nigh unthinkable. Freyer is one of those who glorify war as the essential function of the State. One knows the well-worn maxim that "Politics are but a continuation of war by different means." "During the armistice which we call peace" the State must always keep the return to normal conditions—i.e., war—before its eyes.

Fifteen centuries ago St. Augustine devoted a few chapters of his *De Civitate Dei* to show that all fighting, even that of wild animals and the mythical arch-robber Cacus, had for its object the re-establishment of a state of balance and harmony which he called peace. The achievement of reversing this simple truth that man strives for harmony and not for disharmony, by exalting war as the normal condition, has remained reserved for the sages of the twentieth century.

"The history of man in the age of advanced civilizations is the history of political powers. The form

* H. Freyer, *Der Staat,* p. 146. Leipzig (1925).

this history takes is war, of which peace is a part. It is the continuation of war by different means . . ." * "Man is a predatory animal. When I call man a predatory animal whom do I insult, man or the animal? For the great predatory animals are noble creatures of the most perfect kind without the duplicity of human morality founded in weakness." †

Does not this last Spenglerian dictum, whose echoes are heard in far wider circles than those of Schmitt or Freyer, smack rather of a slightly worn nineteenth-century romanticism? Is there really reason to view the allegedly fundamental fight-impulse in man as an animal trait? Is there an animal that fights for the sake of fighting? Does not it rather fight for that *pax,* that tranquillity of existence which Augustine saw as the principle underlying all cosmic life, from inorganic matter to the heavens above?

All this seemingly profound thinking which passes for realism, because it conveniently does away with all troublesome principles, has a great attraction for the

* Oswald Spengler, *Jahre der Entscheidung,* p. 24.
† *Ibid.,* p. 14. *Cf. Der Mensch und die Technik,* p. 14 ff.

adolescent mind. Now, it is one of the signal characteristics of our time that a large part of humanity no
longer succeeds in outgrowing the confusion of sentiment with understanding typical of the adolescent
age. And it in part is to this confusion that the "life-
philosophy" owes its popularity.

The exaltation of *being* over *knowing* contains
one other consequence worthy of attention. The
repudiation of the primacy of the understanding
means the repudiation of the norms of judgment as
well, and hence the abandonment of all ethical standards. For ultimately every ethical judgment is an act
of discernment. This consequence is fully accepted
by the afore-mentioned writers. We do not judge
civilization, they say, we merely state facts. But
where one has to do with human relationships and
human conduct, the stating of facts can never be
enough and valuation is both imperative and inevitable. In the study from which we have quoted already, C. Schmitt devotes a few remarkable pages to
the concept of evil. He seems inclined to accept the
notion of original sin, that is to say, he professes "that
every genuine political theory * assumes man to be

* He is thinking of Machiavelli and Hobbes.

126

evil." * How does he understand this, however? Thus: Man is "a certainly not unproblematic but dangerous and dynamic being"—a being, therefore, who is apparently entirely at liberty to indulge in his natural wickedness. There you have a completely de-christianised and therefore entirely meaningless definition of evil which vainly chases itself about within the vicious circle of the writer's thesis.

Why do the apostles of the "life-philosophy" worry themselves with Christian terms and notions? Were these to have any meaning for them, they would long since have recognised that the theory of the absolute nature of the political, rooted in and governed by the friend-foe opposition, means a defection from the spirit leading far beyond the sphere of a naïve animalism to a Satanism which sets up evil as a beacon and a guiding star for a misguided humanity.

* *Loc. cit.*, pp. 43, 45, 46.

XIII

DETERIORATION OF MORAL STANDARDS

When considering the implications of a doctrine which renounces the intellectual principle as such for the claims of an ultimately unknowable existence, we were brought face to face with the question of the moral foundations of society. Must we, besides admitting a decline of the critical spirit and the critical faculty, also admit the decay of morals? And if so, how does this decay manifest itself?

Here it is necessary first of all to distinguish clearly between morals and morality, theory and practice of a social period. The moralists of all times have always complained bitterly that the morality of their own time was on the decline. They did so not because of statistical evidence of which they had none, but in that they saw that the present was bad they clung to the illusion that the past had been better. Perhaps it was, perhaps it was not. Our age does dispose of a certain amount of comparative statistics, but they go only a short way back in history. The material is limited, it is open to more than one interpretation and affords little basis for scientific conclusions. In so far as the visible facts of public life are concerned, there would seem to be no reason to condemn our time as being of a lower moral average than any previous period. This is not to say that the level of individual morality has risen, but only that the public order of to-day is more effectual in restraining certain forms of popular misconduct than it used to be. This is particularly true of those forms of misconduct which spring directly from inadequate social conditions, such as intemperance and prostitution, for instance.

One of the many questions about which statistics cannot enlighten us is whether or not the average person of to-day is more "honest" than formerly. For obviously it is not the number of convictions for theft, perjury, fraud or embezzlement which is significant in this respect, but the thousand-and-one shades of sincerity and loyalty which necessarily evade the observation of the police and public opinion.

Even less capable of analytical appreciation are the changes in the field of sexual ethics. To condemn (whether on religious or social grounds) the growing number of divorces and the greater sexual promiscuity among the youth of both sexes is barely to touch the surface of the problem. The ethics of sex have gone much further in breaking away from religion than have the precepts of truthfulness and honesty. Nevertheless, sexual morals, no less than these latter, demand the recognition of a criterion deep down in the individual conscience. Without the personal realisation of the individual human being that he has to resist a radical vice called "unchastity," society falls a helpless prey to sexual degeneration, with destruction as the inevitable result.

On the whole, comparison with earlier periods of Western civilization would not seem to afford sufficient grounds for speaking of a deterioration of average morality. What have deteriorated, however, and deteriorated very seriously, are the standards of ethics in general, the theory of morals itself. Here there is every reason to speak of a crisis-phenomenon and one which must perhaps be deemed even more ominous than that of intellectual weakening. Whilst to all appearances the average man of to-day behaves no better and no worse than his ancestors, the basis of conviction on which moral sentiments and beliefs are founded has become extremely unstable for all who do not feel themselves bound by a code of ethics revealed and incorporated in a religious faith. For uncountable numbers the Christian code of ethics has lost its absolute and binding validity. Has this falling away of the theoretical foundations of morality entailed the evaporation of all feelings of obligation in the individual soul? It does not seem to be the case. The ethics of Christianity in the depotentiated form in which society has always acknowledged them, continue to rule public and private standards of moral conduct. The law, social life, and business still assume that what is viewed as a "normal" majority observes the moral law. The individual feels himself bound by it without asking himself whether this personal compliance is based on faith, philosophy, social interests, or on any other ground. He tries to behave "decently" for others as well as for himself. It does not occur to him to reason why. Unless, of course, intellectual curiosity raises this question in his mind. And if it does, if he sets out to enquire what his moral code is based on, he runs grave risks of finding himself advised on all sides to abandon his unthinkingly accepted pattern of moral standards. For a long time the moral system has been exposed to three undermining influences: philosophical immoralism, certain scientific systems of thought, and æsthetic-sentimental doctrines. We shall have a word to say about each one of these.

The direct influence of philosophical immoralism, or as it perhaps should be called, anti-moral philosophy, is necessarily restricted to a relatively narrow sphere. Its indirect influence is all the greater, however. Docile as the masses are, the knowledge alone that there are thinkers denying the moral order any philosophical *raison d'être* is sufficient for many to conclude that "there can't be much in this morality business."

Far more powerful in its effects than philosophical immoralism is the relativisation of morals implied in scientific systems like historical materialism and Freudian psychology.

In the Marxist doctrine the domain of moral convictions and obligations can occupy no other place than one of the top shelves of the ideological super-structure which raises itself on the economic organisation of a particular period and which, conditioned as it is by the latter, is destined to change and to disintegrate with it. The ethical ideal here remains subject to the social ideal. It has only relative value, relative in the most literal sense of the word. Even the high principles of comradeship and loyalty to the cause of the proletariat which the Marxist doctrine inculcates in its disciples are ultimately motivated by an interest, a class interest. A primer of morals for the young Soviet worker teaches him the value of loyalty—always within the sphere of the class interest—on the same footing with the propriety and utility of clean finger-nails. Moral valuation, as it would be understood by the Christian, the Moslem, the Buddhist, the Spinozist or Kantian, is completely out of the question here. It is self-evident, moreover, that in its practical effect on the masses, a doctrine of this type must necessarily operate in an only half-understood and debased form.

Among the generations which grew to maturity since the beginning of this century, the Freudian system, whose mythological make-up gives it such a universal appeal and which so readily creates the illusion of explaining everything, has doubtless absorbed vast quantities of moral sentiment in its easily comprehensible notion of sublimation. In spite of the fact that it does not absolutely preclude a certain independence of the spirit, Freudianism is essentially even more anti-Christian in its implications than the ethical theory of Marxism. For, in setting up the infantile appetites as the basis of all life of the soul and the spirit it ranges virtue—to speak in Christian terminology—under sin, it places the ultimate origins of the recognition of the highest values in the flesh.

It must be repeated that the author does not here permit himself to pass judgment on the merits of psycho-analysis as a working hypothesis or a therapeutic principle. But just as at an earlier point Freudianism was shown to have done much to weaken the critical standard in the intellectual field, so it appears that it has contributed considerably towards the uprooting of morals from the soil of conscience and well-founded conviction.

Strictly speaking, the æsthetic factor, the last mentioned of the three factors which have been undermining the moral system of Christianity, precedes
the other two. Its influence is already noticeable in
the eighteenth century. Simultaneously with the
weakening of the basis of moral conviction through
the waning of religious belief, a process of dissolution through æsthetic and sentimental reactions sets
in. Literature discovered the lack of reality in the
current representations of virtue and heroism. With
the new veneration of virtue, now thought firmly
secured on rational and social foundations, the need
was felt to subject its quality to more rigorous tests.
A certain realisation of the co-responsibility of social
conditions for crime and vice began to make itself
felt. Literary men begin to exculpate the Gretchens
and Manon Lescauts. As the romantic mood gains
ground the romantic veneration of virtue is blended
with a romantic depreciation of virtue. Virtue and re-
spectability, so long the objects of praise, become out-
moded; they are felt as a source of embarrassed
shame. With the peculiar logic proper to the growth
of a literary *genre,* interest is shifted more and more

from virtue rewarded to evil-doing unpunished. When subsequently the other anti-moral forces towards the end of the nineteenth century begin to exercise a growing influence, literature gets further and further away from the ethical point of view. The abolition of censorship left it free to allow itself anything and everything. To keep a hold on its public a literary *genre* must go on surpassing itself until it collapses. Literary realism sought its task in increasing degree in the unveiling first of the human and the natural, later also of the perverse. It cannot be said that in so doing it assumed the function of that literature of obscenity which had been in more or less secret existence from time immemorial. But meanwhile a large and, in a way, artless public grew accustomed to excesses of literary licence, willing to tolerate them because it had been taught to associate the idea of art with them.

It is an open question whether and to what extent the abandonment of moral standards in literature exercises a direct corruptive influence on the reading public. While one may sometimes feel astonishment at what the youth of both sexes is reading to-day, the impartial observer will nevertheless find himself bound to admit that the studied repudiation of all ethical principles and the coquetting with crime with which literature often regales its public, do not seem to arouse any noticeable desire in the younger generation to shape itself after the literary pattern. Even that certain show of express immorality which might be traced back to literary influences would seem to be out of fashion to-day.

A few words may here be said about the film. It is accused of many crimes. It is said to stimulate unhealthy instincts, to promote criminality, to corrupt the popular taste, to inspire reckless cultivation of the pleasure-seeking impulse. Against this it can be argued that the film, far more than literary fiction, maintains in art the old and popular norms of ethical judgment. The film must be rated a morally conservative factor. If it does not always demand that virtue be rewarded, it will have unrewarded virtue's grief bemoaned. When it vindicates the evildoer it takes away the corrupting effect of such vindication by focusing on the comical element or by the introduction of the sentimental element of sacrifice for love's sake. For its heroes it demands compassionate affection and it rewards them with a happy ending, indispensable culminating effect of all true romanticism. Briefly, the film cherishes a solemn and popular moral order unperturbed by philosophical or other doubts.

Perhaps it will be said that it does all this merely for box-office considerations. These considerations, however, are determined far more by the demands of the public than by the threatening scissors of the censor. It may be concluded, therefore, that the film's moral code still corresponds to the requirements of the popular conscience. This is of importance inasmuch as it affords partial proof that the multiform subversion of moral theory has yet done little to affect the essential moral sentiments of the public at large. Presently we shall see how far this proof goes.

The new will to exalt *being* and *living* over *understanding* and *valuing* appears, therefore, against the background of ethical disarray. This will, which scornfully rejects guidance by the intellect, can find no guidance in a type of ethics which knows itself to be founded in "knowledge." But what then remains to guide and direct this will if guidance is no longer sought in a metaphysical belief centred on an extramundane and incorporeal weal, nor in truth-seeking thought, nor in an all-embracing and generally recognised moral order containing such values as justice and charity? As ever, the answer must be: Only life itself, blind and inscrutable life. The repudiation of all spiritual foundations which the new attitude entails goes much further than its advocates themselves seem to realise.

The general deterioration of the moral principle shows itself rather more in the tendency of modern society to tolerate, to condone, and to acclaim, than in a changed standard of individual conduct. In so far as violence, deception, and cruelty, of which there is more in the world than there used to be, find expression in individual action, this can often be traced to the residue of demoralisation and exasperation left over from the World War and its aftermath of hate and misery. The general deterioration of the moral sense of values can best be observed, therefore, in those countries which have been least affected by the world-wide political and economic upheaval. This deterioration appears most clearly in the appreciation of political conduct as contrasted with the judgment of economic conduct. In respect to moral failings of an economic nature, offences against commercial good faith, abuse of property rights, etc., the popular attitude remains much as it used to be: sincere condemnation with now and then a tolerant smile. The tolerance increases and becomes coupled with a measure of admiration in proportion to the scope of the offence. The international swindler meets with more sympathy than the embezzling clerk from the suburbs. Into the attitude towards the great financial scandals creeps a certain admiration for the talent with which the gigantic machine of technical organisation and international finance is operated. On the whole, however, the moral valuation of economic crime seems to have remained essentially unchanged.

The situation is entirely different when the party forming the object of judgment belongs to and acts in the name of Government. In its attitude towards political conduct—that is, acts committed by the State or any one of its organs—the public at large shows itself increasingly indifferent to moral judgment. Except, of course, when the acting party is a foreign State or an opposition element within the State which has from the outset been branded as "enemy." Still, the tendency of the public to acclaim and admire great political actions is not limited to the acts of the State to which it owes allegiance, alone. The worship of success, which was already seen to exercise a mitigating influence on the judgment of economic misconduct, is capable of eliminating practically all moral indignation from political judgment. It is carried to such lengths that many seem prepared to value a political organisation whose fundamental doctrines they abhor, according to the degree of success with which it achieves its predetermined aim. Incapable of judging the nature of this aim, the means with which it is pursued, and the degree to which it is actually achieved, the spectator contents himself with the external signs of achievement, which are the only ones the newspaper reader or the tourist can observe. Thus a political system which first filled him with disgust and subsequently with fear and awe, will gradually obtain his acceptance and even admiration. Injustice, cruelty, restraint of conscience, oppression, falsity, dishonour, deceit, violation of law and equity?—But look how they have cleaned up the cities and what wonderful roads they have built!

It is no accident that many think to find in an increase of outward order and efficiency the obvious justification of violence and injustice. Order and efficiency have always been the most directly visible signs of a properly functioning political organism. But sound sleep alone is not enough to prove an easy conscience!

XIV

REGNA REGNIS LUPI?

"THE State can do no wrong." So runs a political theory which at present enjoys a popularity extending far beyond the sphere of the Modern Despotism. The State, according to this view, cannot be considered bound by the moral standards of human society. All attempts to submit it to the verdict of ethical judgment must break down on the absolute independence of the political as such. The State stands outside all ethics. One might ask: above all ethics too? Perhaps the theorist of the amoral State will avoid affirming this. He will take recourse to the construction we have already met with at an earlier point, the construction of the political as an absolute category solely governed by the friend-foe opposition, that is to say by an opposition which merely expresses danger and obstruction and the striving to eliminate them. For as we have pointed out before, "friend" in this opposition means no more than potential foe. The State must be solely judged, therefore, by its achievements in the exercise of Might.

Though the particular construction is novel, the theory of the amoral State itself is anything but new. With more or less justification it can be said to derive from thinkers like Machiavelli, Hobbes, Fichte and Hegel. In history itself the theory finds seemingly valuable support. For it is true that history shows little else than greed, lust for power, self-interest, and fear, as the motives governing the actions of States against and amongst each other. The age of systematised absolutism summed up all such motives under the term *"raison d'état."*

In former centuries the contrast between political practice and Christian theory could still easily be effaced and absorbed in the illusion that the acts of the State, however violent and covetous, in ultimate instance remained directed towards defence of the faith, the authority of the Church, the divine right of kings, or Christian justice. The political thought of these older periods, with its rather simple and crude notions, readily accepted these high-sounding representations. Those unable to raise themselves to the required degree of optimism took refuge in another view which enabled them to maintain their belief in the ethical character of the State as such. They viewed the perennial tragedy of violence and injustice as the sinful work of a State which failed to sanctify itself. Under this aspect, too, the principle that States and Governments owed the sacred duty to live after the precepts of religion and justice remained unimpaired. The State could not be permitted to dissociate itself from morals.

As political thought shifted its attention from general principles to the observation of reality and lost its susceptibility to the cruder illusions, a new conception of international order grew up on the foundations of ancient political philosophy, Christian ethics, the code of chivalry, and juridical theory. This point of view was one which, detached from the faith as such, regarded the nations as the members of a community in duty bound to observe the same mutual respect and rules of conduct as law demands from individual members of a community of human beings. Grotius gave this system the classical form which in our time serves as a shining example for those who are striving to lay the foundations of a sound international order.

Both the Christian and the juridical grounds for a moral law and a code of duty for the State are emphatically denied by the theorists of political amorality. It is not only the exponents of Fascist theories who take this attitude. Among historians especially it is often met with. In this connection I may be permitted to quote a few statements of Gerhard Ritter, the significance of which is all the greater for the fact that they come from the lips of this eminent, dispassionate historian. At the time of the Reformation, Ritter says, Germany "was still far removed from the recognition of the preordained ('*naturnotwendig*') autonomy of political life in respect to the Church and the traditional Church doctrine of morals." The German Principalities still lacked "the conscience of the moral autonomy of the secular State." Finally, towards the close of the article, it is stated that the ideas "that all political striving for power has to justify itself before a divine Ruler of the world, that such striving finds its absolute limit in the idea of an eternal law set by God, and that the comity of European peoples, over and above all conflicting national interests, form a community based on Christian morals, are all essentially mediæval-Christian thoughts. If these age-old traditions so far have not yet completely disappeared from English politics, if they there continue to make themselves felt in secularised form while the great Continental nations generally admit the purely biological (*'naturhaft'*) character of all striving for worldly power without any great qualms of conscience, this is due to the confessional struggle which has done so much to mould the spiritual attitudes of the European peoples and to differentiate them from one another." *

To the politically Left-thinking sociologist Karl Mannheim the amoral character of the State appears

---

* *"Die Ausprägung deutscher und westeuropäischer Geistesart im konfessionellen Zeitalter,"* Historische Zeitschrift, 149 (1934), p. 240 (address to the International Historical Congress at Warsaw, August, 1933). This quotation has given rise to an interesting exchange of letters with Professor Ritter in which the latter has made it clear to me that the term "moral autonomy" should not be understood as implying an unqualified acceptance of the amoral State on his part, and furthermore, that he regards the persistence of mediæval conceptions of "eternal right" in English political thought rather as a superiority over Continental ideas than as a sign of backwardness.

as a matter of course. Referring to Friedrich Mein-ecke's *Die Idee der Staatsraison,* he speaks of the "moral tension" which has arisen in the minds of many thinkers, "when they discovered that for the external relations of States Christian and social ethics *do not apply*." * According to Mannheim the process by which this discovery came about was "that all those strata which were in any way connected with Govern-ment had gradually to persuade themselves that any means, however immoral, can legitimately be re-sorted to for the seizure and preservation of sovereign authority." † As we have already indicated, the grow-ing "democratisation" of society will in the end fa-miliarise all classes with these "State morals." "Hith-erto the ethic of plunder has been consciously admis-sible only in marginal cases and had been confined to the ruling groups. But so far from this element of violence and the ethic on which it rests waning with the democratisation of society, it becomes the publicly acknowledged philosophy of the whole so-ciety." Mannheim recognises the extreme danger of

* The italics are mine. Note how the ethical norm is here *a priori* eliminated.

† *Loc. cit.,* page 38.

this "assumption of a political attitude by all strata of society." "When the masses are clearly given to understand that plunder is the basis and the governing principle of all State-building and all external relations between States, and that through internal plunder also entire groups can be deprived of their social functions and the fruits of their labour," it is the end of the ethical element in labour and its steadying influence on society. Mannheim reveals here an alarming consequence of the theory of political amorality, to wit, that this theory cannot remain the exclusive property of the State, that smaller quasi-public groups will also help themselves to it and adapt it to their ends.

Where serious scientific judgment reaches such dismal conclusions it is not surprising that the voice of practical politics should sound an even more ominous note. On the occasion of the solemn installation of a new chair for German law, the Reich Commissioner for Justice is reported by the Press to have stated "that it was not true that one could make politics by appealing to a certain idealistic justice. It was high time to have done with the ludicrous theory that anything less than the hard necessity of assuring the position of the State could determine what is and what is not justice. The earth belongs to the heroic, not to the decadent!" Away, all you decadents, who since Plato have filled the world with your futile prattle!

The State, then, according to these views, may do anything and everything. No falsehood, no deception, no breach of trust, no cruelty, whether against outsiders or nationals, can be held against it as wrong when it serves its own ends thereby. It may combat the enemy with any means useful to its purpose and go to any lengths, including such fiendish extremes as bacterial warfare. Incidentally, in my early years at school the geography textbooks taught that only certain of the most primitive peoples made use of poisoned arrows, and that this custom goes out at a slightly higher level of civilization. I wonder whether this is still to be found in the school books of to-day. If so, it would seem high time we revised either the school books or ourselves.

For the State there can be no question of political misdemeanours or crimes which it could commit. In theory this should apply to the enemy State as well.

The enemy State also should be immune to moral judgment and condemnation. But here the pitiful debility of these ideas about the State, full as they are of the corrupt odours of human greed and folly, immediately reveals itself. In practice this pompous theory of the State standing outside all morality holds solely for one's own State. For as soon as hostility grows acute the cool lofty voice of reasoned argument changes to a hysterical screeching which eagerly grasps insinuation and defamation of the enemy from the old arsenal of virtue and sin: the enemy's mendacity, his duplicity, his cruelty, his diabolical cunning!—But is not the enemy a State too?

There can be no political obligation to foreigners. There is no such thing as political honour either, in so far as honour means loyalty to one's ideals. Where both obligation and honour are lacking trust and confidence must be absent too. *Regna regnis lupi,* the State a wolf unto the State. It is not a pessimistic lamentation like the old *homo homini lupus,* but a positive creed and political ideal. Now it is unfortunate for this theory that every community, even one of animals, is based on mutual trust of beings which *could* destroy one another. Without mutual trust a community of human beings or States is impossible. A State which emblazons the "Do not trust me" on its shield, which is what the theorists of the amoral State would actually have it do, could only exist in a like-minded world by maintaining an absolute superiority of power over all other States combined. Thus the logic of absolute national autonomy leads back to the chimera of a political universalism.

Of all the dangers threatening Western civilization this doctrine of the moral, or better the amoral, autonomy of the State is no doubt the greatest, as it concerns the most powerful factor in human society which can make or break the world at will. It entails the inevitable consequence of mutual destruction or general exhaustion and degeneration of the units in which civilization reposes, the national States. It moreover threatens these units with disintegration from within, in view of the certainty that any group thinking itself strong enough to gain by violence will arrogate to itself that very State character which is the key to the freedom from all obligations to others. In the wake of the amoral supremacy of the State, therefore, follow anarchy and revolution.

The arbitrary decision as to what is the State's interest and how it is to be pursued will always have to be taken by those who are called the leaders. The oath by which their followers are pledged to them, however, will never reach further than the measure of confidence in their political wisdom. Where there is a difference of opinion within the ruling group and the split assumes such proportions that each of the two factions feels itself called upon to force its views through, the strongest or the most active must restrain or exterminate the other. In this form, too, the practice of *coups d'état* and palace revolutions follows inevitably from the logic of the absolute State.

Inasmuch as the theory of the amoral State contains the denial of every principle of truth, honour and justice as *universal* human principles, consistency would require the converts to this theory deliberately to renounce Christianity. They do not do so, however, at least not unanimously and unconditionally. They hold, with Tartuffe: *"Il est avec le ciel des accommodements,"* arrangements which they sometimes try to impose on their particular heaven in a rather heavy-handed fashion. We have here a remarkable instance of what we have called the ambivalence of modern thought or, to put it in more homely terms, a large-scale attempt at eating one's cake and having it. A political theory is proclaimed which is in direct conflict with Christianity as well as with any moral philosophy which preserves the notion of an immutable moral law founded in conscience. At the same time the intention is professed to maintain the Church and Church doctrine, albeit in the mutilated form which the strait-jacket of the totalitarian State will allow.

This attitude shows a very real difference with that of earlier ages. From the sixteenth century until well into the nineteenth the national States have not in general conducted themselves with any greater degree of morality in their relations to one another than to-day. Meanwhile they refused to allow any aspersions on their Christian character; in fact, they even proclaimed it as governing their actions. All this no doubt comprised a large measure of hypocrisy, a hypocrisy which was no less reprehensible because it spoke with the voice of a political community rather than with that of one personal conscience. Nevertheless, political conduct continued to be governed by one universal precept and where practice was too clearly at variance with the ideal, public opinion did not refrain from censuring the acts of the State as unjust.

The position which the State professing its own amoral character arrogates to itself to-day is a very different one. As State it claims absolute autonomy and independence in respect to all moral standards. In so far as it allows the Church and religion, with their explicit and binding moral code, to carry on an existence of their own, their position is no longer one of freedom and equality but of subjugation and compulsory allegiance to the doctrine of the State itself. It is clear that only those devoid of all religion will be able to embrace an ethical system of such glaring ambiguity.

But, the realist thinker will ask, what then would you propose as a universally valid moral standard for political conduct holding out any hope of observance? Do you really believe that as long as international complications remain, the national States will ever behave as good little boys to one another? No, indeed, history, sociology and the knowledge of human nature forbid us to believe it. States will continue to set their course of action predominantly by their interests or what they think to be their interests, and considerations of international morality will drive them only a fraction of an inch off this course. But this fraction represents the difference between honour and loyalty and the jungle, and as such reaches further than a thousand miles of ambition and violence.

The prophets of the amoral State forget, I think— and this is the answer to the question put above— that characteristic of modern thought which permits us to see things in their "antinomic" determination, which compels us to temper every final conclusion with an "and yet . . ." The State is an entity which, given the imperfection of all that is human, will with a seeming inevitability conduct itself according to other norms than those of a social morality based on mutual trust, let alone those of Christian religion. And yet it will never be able completely to discard all principles of Christian or social ethics without incurring the ultimate penalty of perishing in the consequence of such action.

REGNA REGNIS LUPI?

The prophetess of the "Edda" sang:

> *"Wind time, wolf time,*
> *—ere the world will pass,*
> *No man on earth*
> *—his fellow-man will spare."*

But we *will* not perish!

XV

HEROISM

Nᴇʟsᴏɴ's famous signal before the Battle of Trafalgar was not: "England expects that every man will be a hero." It said: "England expects that every man will do his duty." In 1805 that was enough. It should still be. It was enough also for the dead of Thermopylæ whose epitaph, the most beautiful ever conceived, contained nothing but the immortal: "Stranger, make known to the Lacedæmonians that we lie here, to their word obedient."

The active political organisations of to-day make an appeal for all the forceful ideas and noble sentiments to which Trafalgar and Thermopylæ bear testimony: discipline, service, loyalty, obedience, sacrifice. But the word duty does not suffice them for their appeal and they hoist the flag of heroism. "The principle of Fascism is heroism, that of bourgeoisie, egoism." Thus read the election posters which in the spring of 1934 adorned the streets of Italy. Simple and striking like an algebraic equation. An established truth and a creed.

Humanity has ever needed a vision of a higher faculty in man, of human strength and courage in increased potency, as a support and a solace in the hard struggle of life and as an interpretation of greatness in action. Mythological thought placed the realisation of these visions in the sphere of the superhuman. Heroes were demi-gods like Heracles, Theseus. At a later period of Hellas's glory the term comes to be applied to ordinary human beings as well; those who had fallen for their country and the tyrannicides. But always it was the dead. The essence of the heroical idea was worship of the dead. The hero-concept was not far removed from that of the blessed in the hereafter. Only much later does it come to be used in reference to the living, and then really only in a rhetorical vein.

In Christian thought the idea of heroism was naturally overshadowed by that of holiness. The chivalrous conception of life of the feudal period filled the concept of knighthood with all the functions of the heroic: noble service merged with Christian duty.

With the Renaissance European thought begins to visualise the great man in a new form. The emphasis is shifted to the qualities of the mind and bearing in society. In the *virtuoso* or *uomo singolare* courage is only one virtue among many, self-sacrifice no longer a predominant characteristic, and success the important thing. As late as the seventeenth century the Spaniard Baltasar Gracián gives the old name *héroe* to a conception of this kind. In the same century the French *héros* acquires a new meaning. The French drama embodies the qualities of the heroic in the tragical hero, while at the same time the wars of Louis XIV give rise to a national hero-worship of military character, expressing itself to the accompaniment of much brass and drums and wallowing in pompous decoration and bombastic language.

In the eighteenth century the vision of the great man changes once again and loses its homogeneity. Racine's heroes have become those of Voltaire, little more than puppets. The rising democratic idea finds the illustration of its ideal in the old figures of Roman civic virtue. The spirit of rationalism, science and humanitarianism expresses the ideal in the concept of "genius," *das Genie,* the heroic qualities of which are again different from those of the *virtuoso* of the Renaissance. In the idea of "genius" violent and intrepid action no longer ranks in the forefront. Then the new Romanticism discovers still another type of hero which is soon to outstrip the Greek forms as a suggestive image: the Germanic and the Celtic hero. For the spirit which had been caught by the fascination of the primeval, the archaic, vague, truculent and sombre qualities of these fantasies exercised an irresistible attraction. It remains highly remarkable that the hero-concept of modern times takes its cue from the three-quarters false and yet so important product of Macpherson.

All through the nineteenth century the representation of the heroic has been but to a small extent a model and an ideal after which to shape oneself. The "be like these" which had spoken clearly in the ideal of chivalry grew weaker and weaker as the heroic vision came to be increasingly the product of the historian's craving for images of the past. The Germanic heroes emerged from the studies of scholars who had rendered the old poetry and history accessible without themselves taking Siegfried or Hagen as their model of perfection.

The spirit of the nineteenth century as it manifested itself in utilitarianism, political and economic liberty, democracy and liberalism, was but little inclined to the formulation of superhuman standards. Nevertheless, the idea of heroism continues to be further developed, this time in an Anglo-Saxon form.

The Byronic storm had come and gone when Emerson took up his pen. His conception of the heroic is only partly a reaction against the spirit of his time. It is a cultured, optimistic, polished ideal, fully compatible with the ideas of progress and humanity. With Carlyle the element of protest is more pronounced, although there too the strong emphasis on ethical and cultural values divests the heroic conception of the features of wild vehemence and ruthless striving. His *Hero Worship* could, after all, hardly be called a fiery predication or the groundwork of a cult. The social limitations of the Anglo-Saxon art of living left ample room for a heroic ideal cultivated in a literary form in the tracks of Ruskin and Rossetti.

Jacob Burckhardt, who saw the shortcomings of his age more clearly and rejected them more emphatically than anyone else, curiously enough did not make use of the terms heroic and heroism in his reconstruction of the Renaissance-man. His was a new vision of human greatness adding more passionate traits to the genius-idea of the eighteenth century. Burckhardt's admiration for bold action and self-reliant determination by the individual of his life's aims, cut straight across all democratic and liberalist ideals. But he never attempted to present his vision of the heroic as a moral or a political programme. His attitude towards the public was the disdainful aloofness of the solitary individualist. With all his veneration of the energetic, Burckhardt was too much of an æsthetic thinker to create a modern ideal of practical heroism. He was, moreover, too critical to accept and encourage the element of mythical cult forming an integral part of any heroism. When dealing with *"Die historische Grösse"* in his *Weltgeschichtliche Betrachtungen,* he always uses the designation *"das grosse Individuum,"* and not the terminology of heroism.

At one point, however, he has helped to prepare the modern idea of heroism. For he concedes the great man forming part of his vision of the Renaissance, practical dispensation from the moral law without interpreting this exemption philosophically.

Nietzsche's ideas about the supreme human potentialities developed out of an intellectual turmoil such as the tranquil contemplative mind of his master Burckhardt had never known. Through the complete despair of the value of life, Nietzsche comes to proclaim his heroic ideal. It was conceived by a mind which had completely detached itself from the practical realities of political organisation and human society, the idea of a visionary for poets and sages, not for statesmen and ministers.

There is something tragic in the fact that the degeneration of the heroic ideal finds its origin in the shallow popularity of Nietzsche's philosophy which it achieved in the '90s. The poet-philosopher's thought, born of despair, was appropriated by the public at large before it had passed the tests of pure thinking. The man in the street of the '90s spoke of the "superman" as if he were a big brother. This premature vulgarisation of Nietzsche's ideal has doubtless been the beginning of the trend of thought which in our day has made heroism its motto and its programme.

In the process of popularisation the heroic ideal has suffered a bewildering reversion which deprives it of all its deeper meaning. The honorary title of "hero," though at times rhetorically applied to the living, had always remained reserved for the dead just as the attribute "saint." It was the reward of gratitude which the living bestowed on the dead. One did not set out to be a hero but to do one's duty.

Since the rise of the various forms of popular despotism, heroism has become the catchword. Heroism is a political tenet, it is even represented as the new ethic replacing the old which so many think no longer necessary or useful. It would be folly to reject out of hand the value of this sentiment. One must test its veracity and its meaning.

The enthusiasm for the heroic is the most telling sign of the great revulsion away from *knowing* and *understanding* to direct *experiencing* and *living* which we have called the focal point of the cultural crisis. Glorification of action as such, drugging of the critical faculty by over-stimulation of the will, clouding of the idea through a sublime illusion: these are all qualifications which must appear to the believer in the anti-noetic attitude towards life as so many justifications of heroism.

The positive value of this heroic attitude, systematically fostered by the forces of authority in the interests of the State, cannot be denied. In so far as heroism means a stronger personal consciousness of being under obligation to give one's full self to the realisation of a common aim, heroism is an asset to any age. The inherent poetical element of the hero-concept is doubtless of great value in this connection. It imparts to the acting individual that particular tension and exaltation in which great things are done.

It is beyond doubt that modern science, which has made life so much safer than before, has at the same time greatly raised the general level of day-to-day defiance of danger. How Horace, who sang of sea-faring in a ship as the most dauntless tempting of the gods, would have shuddered at the aeroplane or the submarine! The willingness without hesitation to expose oneself to intense danger has greatly increased.

There is unquestionably a connection between the rise of aviation and the spread of the heroic ideal. It is not doubtful where this ideal is most truly realised; it is there where least is said about it, in the daily work of the air pilot.

Heroism means going out of bounds. In this world things must go out of bounds from time to time. One comes here again to the point in one's thinking where judgment must remain inconclusive. No one can desire that the world continue to muddle along in every respect in the groove into which imperfect laws and even more imperfect behavior have pushed it. Without heroic intervention no Council of Nicæa, no dethronement of the Merovingians, no conquest of England, no Reformation, no revolt of the Netherlands, no free America. The thing that counts is *who* intervenes, *how* and in the name of *what*. Expressed in medical terms it may well be that our time is in need of heroic treatment, provided it is administered by the proper physician and in the proper manner.

This metaphor at once leads to another view of the modern heroism. Our time needs this tonic because it is weak. The exaltation of the heroic is in itself a

167

crisis phenomenon. It shows that the ideas of service, task and fulfilment of duty no longer exercise the necessary motive power on the public at large. They have to be amplified as through a loud speaker. They have to be reflated, perhaps inflated.

By whom, for what, how? The value of the political heroism is determined by the purity of its purpose and the practice of its conduct. If it is to merit the association with Thermopylæ and the Nibelungen it must be diametrically opposed to all that is hysterical excitement, boasting, barbaric pride, drilling, parade and vanity; to all that is self-delusion, express exaggeration, make-believe and deception. For let no one ever forget that it was precisely in the limitation of permissible means that lay the strength of the most perfect formulation heroism has ever received, that of mediæval chivalry.

The shirt-and-arm heroism of to-day in practice often means little more than a crude assertion of the "we"-consciousness. A particular subject, "we and those with us" called "party," has a corner in heroism and parcels it out to its servants. Such assertions of the "we"-consciousness are sociologically of the highest importance. They are met with in all periods and in every race in the form of rites, dances, cries, chants, badges, etc. If our time has actually lost the desire to understand and to determine its behaviour rationally, it is perfectly natural that it should go back to primitive methods of instilling the sense of strength and unity.

One danger will always remain inalienably attached to the anti-noetic creed of life. The assumption of the primacy of life over understanding necessarily entails, with the abandonment of the criteria of the understanding, the abandonment of moral standards as well. If authority preaches violence the violent will have the floor. One has denied oneself in principle the right to restrain them. And in this principle they will think to find justification for their actions, whatever their cruelty and bestiality. As executors of the heroic task the political tide will only too easily wash up those elements who find in the perpetration of violence the gratification of their animal or pathological instincts. A rigidly disciplined military authority may perhaps keep them within certain bounds. In the fanaticism of a popular movement, however, they will become the henchmen of murder.

XVI

PUERILISM

WITH a word whose depth surpasses all logical understanding, Plato once called men the playthings of the gods. To-day one might say that man everywhere uses the world as his plaything. Though the latter statement is much less profound, it is yet more than a superficial lamentation.

Puerilism we shall call the attitude of a community whose behaviour is more immature than the state of its intellectual and critical faculties would warrant, which instead of making the boy into the man adapts its conduct to that of the adolescent age. The term has nothing to do with that of infantilism in psychoanalysis. It is based on the observation of evident cultural and sociological facts. We shall not attach any psychological implications to it.

Examples of current uses demanding the qualification of puerilism abound. The *Normandie* makes its maiden voyage and returns from its triumphal journey with a certain blue ribbon. Noble rivalry of nations, astonishing achievement of science! Shipbuilders, shipping companies, maritime specialists all agree that giant liners are impracticable in every respect. In winter the *Normandie* is laid up; it would not pay to run her. Thus one returns to the practice of early mediæval shipping. The sailor's heart sickens to think that this floating palace should be called a ship. That the power of creation embodied in this achievement is impressive, yes, even inspiring, no one with any eye for modern culture will be able to deny. In the tremendous dimensions lies a beauty like that of the Pyramids; beauty there is also in the refined internal efficiency. But the spirit who commanded all this did not strive to express majesty or eternity. All that man has achieved here in calculated transformation of nature merely goes to serve an empty purpose, to play a game which has nothing in common with culture or wisdom and which lacks the high values of play itself because it refuses to be taken as such.

Or take that other game masquerading as business, that game of political ninepins, of continually overthrowing governments on purposely elicited conflicts of party intrigue whereby some great countries, entangled in the rules of a parliamentarianism whose true nature they have never grasped, deprive themselves of the chance of a real purification and strengthening of their system of government. Or think of the renaming of old cities after national figures of the day like Gorki and Stalin.

Let us make only a passing allusion to that spirit of drilling and parading which has engulfed the world. The multitudes are massed together, no square is large enough to hold them, a whole nation stands rigidly at attention like millions of tin soldiers. Even the foreign onlooker is unable to escape the fascination of this spectacle. This seems greatness, power. It is childishness. An empty form creates the illusion of a serious and worthy purpose. Those who can still think know that all this has no value whatever. It merely shows how closely the popular shirt-and-arm heroism is related to a general puerilism.

The country where a national puerilism could be studied most thoroughly in all its aspects, from the innocent and even attractive to the criminal, is the United States. Only one should be careful to approach it with an open mind. For America *is* younger and more youthful than Europe. Much that here would deserve to be qualified as childish is there merely naïve, and the truly naïve guards against any reproach of puerilism. Besides, the American himself is no longer blind to the excesses of his youthfulness. Did he not give himself Babbitt?

The modern puerilism shows itself in two ways. On the one hand, activities of a professedly serious nature and universally regarded as serious, like those mentioned above, come to be permeated with the spirit of play and to bear all the characteristics of play; on the other, activities admittedly of a play-character come to lose the true quality of play because of the manner in which they are carried on. To these latter belong the hobbies and pastimes which assume the weight of international interests with congresses, special newspaper columns, professional experts, manuals, and theories. They should, of course, not be considered on the same level with that particularly striking but superficial symptom of general puerilism, the so-called crazes with their rapid world-wide popularisation like the cross-word puzzle of a few years ago.

It goes without saying that in speaking of these hobbies and pastimes we are not thinking of sport. It is true that physical exercises, hunting and athletic contests are pre-eminently manifestations of youthfulness of human society. But this type of youthfulness is a different thing from puerilism. Without competition there can be no culture. That our time has found in sport and sporting events a new international form of gratifying the ancient agonistic impulse is perhaps one of the factors which may contribute most towards the preservation of our culture. Modern sport is in no small measure a gift to the world from England, a gift of which this world has learned to make a better use than is the case with the other things that England gave, such as parliamentary government and trial by jury. The new cult of physical strength, of skill and courage, for both sexes, is in itself a positive cultural factor of the greatest value. Sport gives vitality, zest for life, balance and harmony, all of inestimable worth for culture.

This should not blind us to the fact that modern puerilism has also found its way into sport. It is present wherever athletic rivalry assumes proportions tending to push intellectual interests into the background, as is the case at some American universities. It threatens to creep in with over-organisation of sport and with the disproportionate place which the sporting page and the sporting magazines have come to occupy in the mental diet of untold numbers. It shows itself in a particularly striking form where national passions impede the observance of fair play in international contests. In general, sport is capable of temporarily effacing national antagonisms. It is only too well known, however, that this rising above the desire for national glory is not always what it should be, as for instance in those cases where the fear of public commotion curbs the arbiter's independence of judgment. With the acerbation of national feeling the chances of such degeneration become progressively greater. Being a bad loser has always rightly been called childish. A whole nation which shows itself a bad loser deserves no other qualification.

If modern society must indeed be held to exhibit a marked degree of puerilism the question arises whether it shares this characteristic with earlier

civilized periods, and if so, whether it compares un-
favourably with these latter in this respect. It could
easily be shown that erstwhile society often conducted
itself in a manner which can only be qualified as immature. There would, nevertheless, appear to be a
difference between the immaturities of the past and
the childishness of to-day.

In the more incipient phases of civilization a large
part of social life is carried on in the form of play,
that is to say, within an artificial mental sphere governed by rules of its own and temporarily encompass-
ing all conduct in a voluntarily accepted system of
action. A conventional proceeding takes the place
of the direct pursuit of utility or pleasure. Where
the play is holy this activity becomes a cult or a rite.
Even if the rites or contests involve bloodshed the
action still remains play. All such play requires a
local limitation, the creation of a playground shut
off from the world outside. Ordinary life is excluded
from these precincts for as long as the play lasts. The
old Greek *temenos,* the lists of tournament, the stage
of a theatre, the ring, are such sacred circles of play.
The reality outside the playground is forgotten, there
is a general surrender to the common illusion, free

judgment is set aside. All true play still bears these features.

The most fundamental characteristic of true play, whether it be a cult, a performance, a contest, or a festivity, is that at a certain moment it is *over*. The spectators go home, the players take off their masks, the performance has ended. And here the evil of our time shows itself. For nowadays play in many cases never ends and hence is not true play. A far-reaching contamination of play and serious activity has taken place. The two spheres are getting mixed. In the activities of an outwardly serious nature hides an element of play. Recognised play, on the other hand, is no longer able to maintain its true play-character as a result of being taken too seriously and being technically over-organised. The indispensable qualities of detachment, artlessness and gladness are thus lost.

To a certain extent something like this contamination has been present in all cultures as far back as we can see. But it is the dubious privilege of modern Western civilization to have given this diffusion of the two spheres of life its greatest intensity. With great numbers of both the educated and the ignorant, the play-attitude towards life of the adolescent has become permanent. At an earlier stage we have already alluded to the prevalence of a state of mind which might be called one of permanent adolescence. It is characterised by a lack of sense of decorum, a lack of personal dignity and of respect for others and the opinions of others, and an excessive concentration on self. The general weakening of judgment and of the critical impulse has prepared the soil for the spread of this attitude.

Now it is both interesting and disquieting to note that the emergence of this state of mind is facilitated not only by a decreased desire for individual judgment, by the standardising effect of group organisations providing a set of ready-made opinions, and by the ever-available opportunities for trivial diversion, but also by the marvellous development of technical facilities. In his world full of wonders man is like a child in a fairy tale. He can travel through the air, speak to another hemisphere, have a continent delivered in his home by radio. He presses a button and life comes to him. Will such a life give him maturity? On the contrary.

In making mention of the contamination of play and seriousness in modern life, we enter upon a fundamental problem of culture which cannot be investigated in this book.* The phenomenon shows itself partly in a semi-serious attitude towards work, duty, fate and life, partly in the attribution of great importance to what a clear judgment would qualify as trivial, and in the treatment of truly important things with the instincts and gestures of play. Political speeches of leading figures which should properly be described as mischievous pranks are not rare.

It would be interesting to investigate how in the different languages the words for play continually overflow into the sphere of the serious. American English would offer an especially promising field for a study of this kind. The American reporter speaks of his profession as "the newspaper game." The politician who, though by nature honest, finds himself forced to howl with the wolves of corruption, offers as his justification that he had "to play the game." The customs official is implored to close his eyes to an infringement of the prohibition law with

* Note: In the not too distant future I hope to deal with this problem in a separate work.

the words "be a good sport." It is clear that far more is involved here than a mere question of popular speech. It is a fundamental change of a moral-psychological nature.

The semi-serious attitude towards life is characterised by the use of *slogans* as a means of persuasion. In the comparatively recent past the Americans gave to the old Scottish-Irish word for the battle and rallying cry of the clans the meaning of a political password or motto. A slogan, one might say, is a party adage of which those using it know perfectly well that it is only half true and that its purpose is to help the party to power. It belongs to the realm of play.

The Anglo-Saxon peoples, with their highly developed play-instincts, enjoy the privilege of remaining capable of distinguishing the element *fun* and *game* in their actions. Not all races have been equally blessed. The Latin, the Slavonic, and the continental Germanic peoples often seem to be far less well equipped in this respect. What else, for instance, is "Blood and Soil" but a slogan, a maxim which with a suggestive image veils all the defects of its logical foundation and the dangers of its practical application? The slogan, however, which is not recognised as such and instead is made a part of even the official and scientific language of a nation, necessarily becomes twice as dangerous in its potential effects thereby.

The slogan belongs to the field of publicity, whether commercial or political. Now it is one of the fundamental features of all modern publicity, that hypertrophic product of our time, that it is based on this attitude of semi-seriousness characteristic of over-refined civilizations. It is perhaps to be viewed as a symptom of old age. Puerilism is the proper word for it.

This widely prevalent attitude of semi-seriousness at once explains the close connection between heroism and puerilism. The moment the motto becomes "Let us be heroes" a great game has started. It could be a noble game if it were consummated entirely within the sphere of Spartan matches of youths, or the Olympic games. But as long as it is played in the form of political action, in parade and national drill, in oratorical bombast and "officially inspired" newspaper articles, and with all this yet takes itself seriously and demands to be taken seriously, it is truly puerilism.

The confusion of play and seriousness which lies

at the bottom of all that was here classified as puerilism, is no doubt one of the most important aspects of the malady of our time. There remains the question as to how far puerilism is connected with that other trait of modern life, the glorification of youth. The two should be clearly distinguished. Puerilism knows no ages, it attacks young and old alike. The adoration of youth, superficially a sign of fresh strength, may also be viewed as a symptom of old age, an abdication in favour of the coming heir. While most strong cultures have loved and honoured youth they never cajoled or exalted it, and they always demanded from it obedience and respect for its elders. Typically decadent and puerile were the quickly evaporated movements which called themselves Futurism. One cannot say that youth was to blame for them.*

* Two manifests recently given out by the well-known founder of Futurism, F. T. Marinetti, may be recommended as an interesting illustration of what has here been said about puerilism. They can be found, in translation, in the Oct. 1935 and Nov. 1935 issues of the publication *The World* (London), as well as in the *Hamburger Monatshefte für auswärtige Politik,* Nov. 1935, p. 7.

XVII

SUPERSTITION

A RECRUDESCENCE of superstition does not come as a surprise in a time which tends to sacrifice the ideals of knowledge and judgment to the will to live. Always fascinating and suggestive, superstition in times of spiritual turmoil regularly becomes the fashion. It temporarily acquires a certain distinction. It stimulates the imagination and helps us to forget the narrow limitations of our understanding.

This is not the point for a discussion of all the various forms of modern superstition. Only two of them will be indicated. The first lies in the realm of superstitious ideas of which but few people can entirely free themselves, viz., the reluctance to tempt fate. This sentiment has extremely deep roots in the human consciousness. It might be called a disguised belief. How many people do not touch wood to avert a misfortune while they are all the time sincerely convinced that they do not attach any meaning to this practice? Here lies the explanation of the fact that every new danger is accompanied by its own particular form of superstition. In the days when the motorcar was still considered dangerous the mascot swung about against the back window. To-day one hardly ever sees it. On the other hand, it is credibly reported that one of the world's best-known air-transport companies demands from its pilots, in addition to the usual tests and examinations, the production of a horoscope. It is quite natural that aviation, with its highly increased dangers, should have its own particular desire for psychic reassurance. It remains none the less a cause for apprehension that a large official body should honour the rebirth of astrology in this manner. A superstition which pretends to be scientific creates a much greater confusion of thought than one which contents itself with simple popular practices. The horoscope is thought to provide exact information while, assuming that it has any significance at all, it can hardly be more exact than the description on a passport.

The most widespread and pernicious form of modern superstition lies not with a too ready acceptance of mysterious relationships,* nor with an appeal to quasi-science, but entirely within the sphere of purely rational thinking and confidence in true science and technology. It is the belief in the effectiveness of modern war and the instruments of waging it.

There has no doubt been a long period of history in which war as a method could claim a relatively large measure of effectiveness. An Eastern empire of early times could destroy its enemies without worrying about the fact that in the long run the *system* would turn the Near East into a barren wilderness. In European history, also, one can find a number of defensive and one or two offensive wars of unmistakable efficacy. The large majority of wars, however, can hardly be classed as really effective. Think of the Hundred Years War, the wars of Louis XIV, the Napoleonic wars whose effect was cancelled by Leip-

* The author refrains here from any judgment on the value of serious research concerning unexplained psychical phenomena.

zig and Waterloo. In nearly all these instances there is only the effectiveness of the immediate result. The ultimate aim, peace and security, is almost always attained, not through warfare, but through exhaustion.

As the implements of war become more powerful and as the countries able to wage war grow more dependent for their existence on peaceful intercourse, the effectiveness of war declines. The transition from standing armies of mercenaries to conscription and universal compulsory service means an enormous stride towards the inutility of war as a method. The sacrifice of national energy and resources increases a thousandfold. With the firearm the case lies different again. One may say that from its invention to the end of the nineteenth century firearms have augmented the effectiveness of war. Subsequently, with the rapidly increasing power of explosives, the utility curve turns sharply downward. For not only does the sum total of destruction on both sides assume such dimensions that it more than offsets the ultimate gains for the victors, but also where there is any semblance of equal forces, the waste and sacrifice of the fighting itself are out of all proportion to the immediate results achieved. Every weapon has a certain utility only as long as the enemy does not possess it. What is true of explosives holds equally for all the apparent perfections added to the art of warfare by wireless telegraphy, concrete construction, submersion technique, and aviation. Every success obtained through them is an illusory success of only immediate value, usually of no value at all. What else were the great destroyers in the Great War but amulets around Britannia's neck? What have all the gallantry, all young life, and also all the violation of right and all the cruelty of submarine warfare achieved but a prolongation of the struggle?

The world can no longer bear modern war. It can only be mutilated by it. Peace it cannot bring. For the spirit of peoples is so thoroughly mobilised and at the same time so poisoned that every war must leave an enormously increased residue of hate. The final result of the World War could practically be dictated by the victors. The pick of political wisdom assembled at Versailles. And what did they achieve? Crude amputations and new complications more insoluble than before, a brew of misery and demoralisation to come. It is easy enough to denounce the stupidities of Versailles. As if victory on the other side would have brought wiser peacemakers and riper solutions!

And meanwhile we go on sowing dragons' teeth. With the most strenuous efforts of science, technology, and the taxpayer, we are building up armies, navies, air forces, hoping fervently all the time (at least most of us do) that they will never be used. Expressed in terms of pure utility, this is but fabricating scrap-iron.

The persistent belief in the utility of war is a superstition in the most literal sense, a survival from earlier phases of civilization. How is it possible that a man like Oswald Spengler, in his *Jahre der Entscheidung,* can let his imagination run wild with this superstition! From what depths of romantic illusion does his idea of the modern Cæsars with their heroic bands of professional soldiers arise! As if the world of to-day would still be able to control and limit itself in the use of its means and forces!

I see again that small Chinese village with the gate walls covered with strips of red paper bearing sacred formulæ to avert danger and calamities. They doubtless gave the inhabitants a feeling of security. And

188

what else is security but a feeling? How practical and how economical! How much more effective than our terrific expenditure on defence which fails to create a feeling of security. Why is it we call the one superstition and the other sound policy?

The foregoing should not be taken as a plea for unilateral disarmament. We are all in the same boat, from which anyone can only get out at his own peril. Our point here is simply that a belief in means and methods whose ineffectiveness is crystal-clear and beyond all doubt, deserves no other name than that of superstition. It is a dull-witted world which lives in such beliefs. The picture of the boat fits the situation only too well: a boat in which the nations are crowded together, to live or to sink together.

XVIII

ART AND LITERATURE ESTRANGED FROM REASON AND NATURE

As THE first of the long series of crisis-symptoms we took the evolution of scientific thinking beyond the sphere of reason and imagination, leaving mathematical formulæ as its only means of expression. In conclusion let us look at Art. For half a century art also has been getting further and further away from reason. Is the process analogous to that of science?

The poetic art of all times, even when the poet is transported to the highest raptures, always maintains a certain connection with rational expression. Though beauty in imagination is its essence, it expresses this beauty through words, that is to say, as thought, for even the vision suggested with a single word is a thought. The instruments of the poet are the logical implements of speech. However high the imagination may soar, the poem's fabric remains a logically expressed thought. Vedic hymns, Pindarus, Dante, the deepest mystical poetry and the most lyrical love song, they none of them lack the logical and grammatically consistent frame. Even the indeterminateness of Chinese poetry does not seem to invalidate this statement.

There have been times when the reason-content of poetry was exceptionally high. The seventeenth century in France is one of these, culminating in Racine. Taking the French classics as the starting point from which to follow up the relationship poetry-reason, one finds that this relationship undergoes comparatively little change until well into the eighteenth century, when, with the ascent of Romanticism and its powerful inspiration, wide fluctuations begin to appear. The share of the non- and anti-rational grows larger. During a large part of the nineteenth century the form of poetic expression nevertheless remained preponderantly rational. That is to say, through their knowledge of the language and the idea-system even the poetically unreceptive could still understand the formal construction of the poetry of this time. It is not until the closing years of the century that one sees poetry purposely steering its course away from reason. The major poets began to refuse to acknowledge the criterion of logical intelligibility. This is not the point to decide whether this orientation away from reason means a step forward and an ennoblement of poetic art, whether it rendered poetry better able than before to fulfil its fundamental function of penetrating to the essence of things. All that is stated here is the fact of poetry's estrangement from reason. To the poetically unreceptive, Rilke or Paul Valéry must remain far more inaccessible than Goethe or Byron were to their contemporaries of like spiritual qualifications.

The estrangement from reason in poetic art has its counterpart in the turning away from the visible forms of reality in the plastic arts. The *ars imitatur naturam* had for many centuries since its formulation by Aristotle remained an unshakable article of faith. Stylistic, ornamental or monumental treatment of the subject, though it at times seemed to disturb the realisation of this principle, by no means abrogated it. The meaning of the adage, incidentally, was never that art merely *copies* what it sees in nature. Its portent is far deeper: art *imitates* nature, that is, like nature it creates forms. Nevertheless, the perfect reproduction of visible reality always remained a universally cherished ideal. For plastic expression deference to nature in a sense meant deference to reason, inasmuch as reason is the organ with which man interprets his environment and makes it translucent. Thus it is no accident that the art of the same century which shows a certain maximum of reason in poetry should also have gone very far in conforming to nature, as appears most clearly in the Dutch painting of the period.

Throughout the eighteenth century the line of realism in plastic art runs more or less parallel with that of reason in poetry. The change brought by Romanticism in this respect is more apparent than real. For the displacement of the subject from the sphere of day-to-day life to that of the fantastic did not in any way involve the relinquishment of visible reality as the store of forms on which to draw for expression. Delacroix and the Pre-Raphaelites continued to express their fantasies in the language of plastic realism, that is, through the reproduction of

193

what can be observed in visible reality. In Impressionism also there is as yet no abandonment of the forms which the eye perceives and which are known to the mind. It is simply another method to achieve the same effect, although it is true that Impressionism does represent a lessening attachment to the inventory of reality. Nor does the new tendency towards stylistic and monumental treatment mean a break with the old tradition.

It is only when the artist attempts to create forms which are not to be found in reality as it appears to the ordinary eye, that the rupture actually takes place. While sometimes the individual figures in the artistic composition may still have been taken from nature, their grouping is such that the whole no longer corresponds to a logically filtered perception of reality. Odilon Redon can, I think, be considered the principal originator of this phase of art, though in Goya's work, too, there are already signs pointing in this direction. For the moment we may call the form-elements expressed in this manner dream-values. Goya's genius was able to clothe the most "unseeable" things still in the language of natural forms. His successors no longer possessed this ability or refused to exercise it.

The trend of development connecting Goya with Odilon Redon culminates in the work of men like Kandinsky and Mondriaan. With their complete relinquishment of the concrete thing of natural shape as the framework of pictorial expression, the art of painting discards all the ordinary means of the perceptive faculty.

Lack of technical knowledge forbids me to go into the question whether in the field of music the evolution from Wagner to atonalism represents one other instance of the same cultural development which showed itself in the tendencies of poetry and painting.

A certain analogy between the position of art and that of science is undeniable. Scientific thought was seen to be hovering on the frontiers of the knowable. Poetry and plastic art, like scientific enquiry functions of the mind, methods of comprehending life, similarly seem to reach out beyond the sphere of the knowable. The presumption would seem to be that this development of æsthetic expression is characterised by the same inevitability as was found to be inherent in the evolution of scientific thought.

On closer consideration, however, a fundamental difference between the two phenomena reveals itself. Art and science approach this untravelled land in entirely different ways.

In science the spirit, in unconditional obedience and submission to the dictates of the perceptive and critical faculties of the intellect, and under the requirement of utmost exactness, is carried along to heights and depths from which it cannot return. It must needs go ever further. Its path is clearly marked. To follow this path is a voluntarily accepted service to a master called Truth.

In art there is no such external compulsion. There is no duty of exactness. Art (or rather many of its servants) has come to the complete abandonment of the principles of observation and thought by its own volition. The artist seeks surrender to undistilled sensations and reactions which are to be the material of his æsthetic expression. In its progressive defection from the logical, the æsthetic understanding (for such it ultimately remains) has become increasingly vague. The poet desirous of delivering his mind scatters syntactic fragments into space which are senseless in their juxtaposition.

For art there is no absolute imperative. Art is not restrained by a discipline of the mind. Its creative impulse is centred in the will. And here the important fact reveals itself that art stands much closer than science to the modern life-philosophy which sacrifices understanding to life. The new art actually and sincerely thinks to represent and interpret life without making use of the intellectual function, forgetting that such interpretation and its expression none the less remain acts of the mind.

All art is a striving and our over-conscious age demands that such striving be given a name. Recent art movements called themselves Expressionism and Surrealism, to say nothing of senseless designations like Dadaism. Both terms signify that the artist is not content with a simple rendering of what he sees in reality or in imagined reality. Expression is what all art has ever been. Why, then, talk of Expressionism? Unless the word is taken simply as a protest against Impressionism, it must indicate that the artist desires to render the object of his artistic creation (for an object and a rendering there must always be) in its deepest essence, divested of all that is irrelevant to its nature or disturbing to the perception thereof. When the object is a seamstress, or a breakfast table, or a valley, the Expressionist disdains to give a natural rendering of the outward appearance of these objects which would be the most adequate method of conveying the conception as such. He claims to give something more, something that lies behind the visible reality; the essence of the thing. He calls it the idea or the life of the thing, giving us to understand that his way of rendering expresses qualities inaccessible to the thinking mind. He pretends to leap over the noetic domain to the core of the thing itself.

It is clear that in so doing he assumes an attitude very much akin to that of the life-philosophy dealt with earlier. In fact, the terminology of modern art criticism corresponds almost entirely to the wording of the anti-noetic *Weltanschauung*. The following is taken from a review of the work of the artist Chagall:—

"I know it: for many the art of Chagall is a problem. In its essence, however, it is really not problematic at all, it is an art which springs directly from a wondering and from a surrender to the myth of life, without thinking, without intervention of the intellect. It has an underground of religious feeling. There is its source, in the heart, if you will, or in the blood or in the mystery of life itself. It is problematic only for those who cannot do without the æsthetic problem or for those who must think something about what they see, while this art eliminates thought. One may ask why this has been done thus and that so. The answer is silence, for there is no answer. After all, there is still a mystery as well as a mysticism of art, there is an art also with a magic faculty which imparts information, not to the intellect but to all that for which we have but meagre notions. About the whole-hearted surrender to life there can be no dispute. There are only two possibilities: to surrender or not to surrender."

Once the point of view is accepted and the lack of argumentation disregarded, this can be considered a perfectly consistent declaration of faith of the new art.

199

Is this harmony with an at present widely accepted creed of life wholly a source of strength for art? There seems good reason to doubt it. For it is just this assertion of the will and of its good right to absolute freedom which threatens to engulf art in excess and degeneration. The perpetual hankering after originality, which is another of the ailments of our time, renders art much more susceptible than science to all corruptive outside influences. Art lacks not only the discipline of science but also the indispensable isolation of science. In art the profit-making possibilities of the mind play a much larger part than in science. The impulse to compete in the use of technical means, whether for the sake of publicity or simply out of vanity, brings art to the pitiful extremes of senselessness which a decade ago introduced themselves as expression of an idea, such as poems solely composed of natural sounds or mathematical signs and similar absurdities. It need hardly be pointed out how easily art lapses into puerilism, a danger, incidentally, to which science also is anything but immune. The *"épater le bourgeois"* has unfortunately not remained the merry slogan of a truly youthful bohemia. Art is far more susceptible to mechanisation and fashion than science. Thus at one time painters all over the world suddenly begin to set their still lives at an angle of thirty degrees and dress their "Labourers," all suffering from pathological distension of the extremities, in stove-pipes instead of trousers.

The more voluntary character of artistic as compared with scientific endeavour clearly reveals itself in the different positions occupied in art and science by the terms ending in -ism. In scientific thinking the -ism terms are chiefly limited to the domain of philosophy. Monism, vitalism, idealism are terms indicating a general point of view, a philosophical conception with which the work is approached. On the methods of investigation and the results obtained these points of view have little or no influence. Scientific production moves steadily onward without being swayed now by this, then by that -ism. Only when it comes to the philosophical reduction of knowledge to a universal principle do the -isms play their part.

In art the situation is rather different. In the history of art and literature a large number of successive tendencies in artistic production are called by names like manierism, marinism, gongorism, etc. These names never derive from the great artists themselves. The artist of earlier periods did not designate his artistic striving with any particular name; he knew no -isms. It is a pre-eminently modern phenomenon that art begins with proclaiming a movement which it christens as an -ism, and only then attempts to make the corresponding work of art. This self-willed adherence to an -ism no doubt exercises a strong influence on the method of working. The product appears more or less as the result of the -ism, far more than in the domain of science. Thus one may say that the direction followed by art as contrasted with science is to a certain extent determined by the will, the will to paint or to write "thus" or "so."

In another respect, however, æsthetic production shows more resemblance to science than the noisiness of the -isms would imply. For underneath the superficial action and reaction of artistic movements and fashions a great stream of seriously inspired work continues steadily and quietly, without freakish deviations into shallow beds.

XIX

DECAY OF STYLE AND TENDENCIES TOWARDS IRRATIONALISATION

IN THE development of art and literature our æsthetically sensitive generation will best be able to recognise the appearance of the tendencies which have brought our culture to a state of crisis. The æsthetic development reflects, as it were, the physiognomy of the cultural process as a whole; it reveals its unity and shows the evolution of the present crisis as extending over two centuries of European culture.

From this æsthetic point of view the process appears as loss of style. The proud history of the West presents itself to us in a succession of styles. We call them: Romanesque, Gothic, Renaissance, Baroque. In first instance all these names denote special forms of architectural and sculptural creation. The words have overflown into a wider sphere of meaning, however; they are increasingly used to label our vision of the intellectual life, even of the entire structure of the respective periods. Each epoch has thus come to have its particular æsthetic qualification. The eighteenth century appears as the last of these epochs bearing the mark of a general homogeneous quality of style, a style pervading every domain of intellectual and artistic creation, despite all profusion and variation an expression of life as a whole.

If the nineteenth century appears to us in a very different light it is not because we are still too close to it. We know it only too well: the nineteenth century never had a style of its own. At most there was a faint afterglow. Its characteristic is lack of style, mixing of styles, imitation of old styles. The beginning of this process of decay goes back to the eighteenth century. The latter's play with the exotic and the historic already foreshadows the tendency to imitate which subsequently finds clear expression in a style which for this very reason can no longer be called a true style, the "empire."

This evanescence of style as the mark of an epoch

is at the heart of the cultural problem. For the revulsion in art and literature is merely the most apparent aspect of the revulsion of culture as a whole.

It would be absurd, however, simply to identify
this loss of style with a general decay of culture. In
one and the same process culture rises to its highest
level and develops the germs of potential decline.

Towards the middle of the eighteenth century the
great reaction sets in which turned man's spirit away
from the coldly rational towards the mysterious
depths of life itself. Interest turns to all that is direct,
personal, original, intrinsic, genuine, spontaneous;
to all that is unconscious, instinctive and wild. Sentiment and imagination, rapture and dream resume
their place in life and expression. To this intensified
apperception of life which one may label with the
term Romanticism, we owe Goethe and Beethoven,
together with the rise of the sciences of history, philology, ethnology, etc. In this very shift towards life,
however, lay the germs of that trend of thought
which once was to culminate in the disavowal of the
understanding in favour of life.

This was not to be until much later, however.
For with the ascendance of the Romantic attitude,

in the above sense, the spirit of exact analytical enquiry, of observation and experiment, was by no
means obliterated or thrown off its course. On the
contrary, in conjunction with the new Romanticism it gained fresh perspectives and possibilities.
Throughout the nineteenth century the ideals of
knowledge, on a basis of rigorous criticism and conduct directed towards unity and concord which the
Age of Reason had proclaimed, continued to rule
unimpaired.

Viewing the development of the spiritual process
since the middle of the eighteenth century as a whole,
it would appear that in the course of this process sensitive perception has gradually penetrated further
and further into the domain of thought. Æsthetic
and sensitive appreciation infused themselves into
logical understanding. Conversely, in the works of
beauty and feeling the reason element inherent in
their forms of expression grew progressively weaker.
This general process comes to its extreme culminating point when the understanding as such is denied
the primacy as a means for comprehending the
world.

The danger of this irrationalisation lies, above all, in that it is accompanied by the highest development of technical powers. It is clear that the worship of life to which the irrationalisation of culture has given rise, cannot but promote the cult of self. Cult of self, however, means exasperation of the craving for earthly well-being. Now if this craving finds at its disposal the unlimited possibilities of a highly developed technical faculty, the danger to society inherent in any cult of self is greatly increased, since the satisfaction of this craving for well-being must needs lead to the destruction of the well-being of others. It is immaterial in this respect whether the social organisation of the craving for material well-being assumes a capitalist, bolshevist, or fascist form. For it is no better than shallow thinking to assume that collectivism excludes egotism.

We are in the midst, therefore, of what is, to all appearances, the gravest combination of dangers that can threaten civilization. A return to reason and rationalism is not enough to help us out of the whirlpool. The counterweight to the co-operation of destructive factors can only be found in the highest metaphysical and ethical values.

If, then, a retrieval of ethical and metaphysical values is what is needed, it can hardly be said that we are on the right road at present. The sense of human responsibility, seemingly strengthened by the exhortations of heroism, has been uprooted from the soil of the individual conscience and mobilised in favour of any collectivity which desires to impose its will and to elevate its limited insight to a canon of weal, thus greatly increasing the danger of absolutely irresponsible mass action. With the growing worthlessness of the spoken or printed word consequent upon its ever greater distribution which the progress of civilization has made possible, the indifference to truth increases in direct proportion. With the spread of the irrationalistic attitude the margin of misunderstanding in every field is steadily expanding. The immediate publicity engendered by commercial interests and the craving for sensation inflates simple differences of opinion into national hallucinations. The ideas of the day demand immediate results, whereas the great ideas have always penetrated very slowly. Like smoke and petrol fumes over the cities, there hangs over the world a haze of empty words.

XX

PROSPECTS

We were bold enough to call our review of crisis-symptoms a diagnosis. For the conclusions which now have to follow prognosis is too strong a word. The outlook remains shrouded in uncertainty. All we can do is to evaluate certain possibilities, to suppose certain eventualities.

Is there still room for a hopeful conclusion after the enumeration of so many grave manifestations of dislocation and evisceration? Room for hope there is always, but confidence is difficult.

No doubt those who cherish the creed exalting life over understanding can declare that their people are not living in a mood of decline but instead are on the way towards a glorious unfolding of all their strength. To them all the phenomena which filled us with apprehension represent the triumph of the creed which they serve. For us, however, arises the question: If prosperity, order, health, even concord were restored to the world, but the spirit of this creed continued to prevail, would civilization thereby be saved?

We know that the world of to-day cannot turn back. We realised this as soon as we looked at science, philosophy and art. Thought and the creative power must continue undaunted on the road which the mind compels them to follow. But it is no different with technology and its enormous apparatus or with the entire economic, social, and political machine. It is unthinkable that through an express act of intervention one could restrain the ever-more effectual mechanism of knowledge-distribution, that is, popular education, publicity, book production; or that one could obstruct new possibilities of communication, applied science, and utilisation of nature.

And yet this prospect of a civilization left at the mercy of its own intrinsic dynamism, of a still always increasing domination of nature, of still more complete and immediate publicity, possesses the complexion of a nightmare rather than the promise of a purified and improved culture. It evokes only antici- pations of unbearable over-loading and slavery of the spirit. For some time this oppressing anticipation of a steadily expanding apparatus of civilization has been causing us to ask ourselves the anxious question: Is the cultural process through which we are passing one of barbarisation?

Barbarisation may be defined as a cultural process whereby an attained condition of high value is grad- ually over-run and superseded by elements of lower quality. It is open to dispute whether or not the bear- ers of the higher and the lower elements necessarily confront each other as the élite against the masses. In any case the assumption of this polarity requires that the terms *élite* and *mass* are dissociated from their social basis and solely viewed as denoting types of mind, or spiritual attitudes. This, of course, is how Ortega y Gasset has used the terms in his *Revolt of the Masses.*

Our knowledge of general and thorough barbari- sation in the past is limited to only one instance: the decline of ancient civilization in the Roman Empire.

As has already been pointed out in an earlier chapter, however, comparison with the present is hampered by a great difference in circumstances. In the first place the earlier cultural process took up a period of almost five centuries. It was furthermore complicated by facts which do not appear to be present in our time. The internal barbarisation of the world of antiquity was conditioned, among other things, by the following three factors. The first was a failure of the function of the State organism with the consequence of a breakdown of frontiers and finally an invasion by foreign peoples. The second, a recession of economic vitality to a level of lower intensity. The third, the rise of a higher form of religion which became largely indifferent to the old culture and whose solid organisation enabled it to take over the power of regulating the cultural life. In the cultural process of our time there are as yet few, if any, indications of any such technical decay or religious uplifting.

The bulwark of its technical perfection and its powerful economic and political equipment does not in any way safeguard our present civilization against barbarisation. For barbarism can avail itself of every one of these technical perfections. Disposing of such perfections barbarism becomes all the more powerful and despotic.

As an example of a very great technical achievement with the most useful and beneficial possibilities, which nevertheless indirectly threatens to impair culture, is the wireless. No one will doubt for a moment the extraordinary value of this new instrument of communication. S O S messages, music and news for the isolated in remote places, are only a few of its manifold blessings. And still, as an organ of information, wireless in its everyday function means in many respects a regression to a less effective form of transmission of thought. We are here not thinking of the recognised evils of popular practice: listening-in without listening or the fatuous shiftlessness which degrades the business to a messing about with sound and thought. Apart from all these not unavoidable defects, the wireless constitutes a slower and more restricted form of knowledge-assimilation. For the pace of our time the spoken word is much too cumbersome. Reading is the higher cultural function. In reading the mind absorbs much more quickly; it is perpetually selecting, it braces itself, skips, stops to think; it exercises a thousand mental activities denied to the listener. In an article entitled *The Decline of the Written Word* an advocate of film and wireless in educational instruction predicted with glad assurance a near future in which the child would be brought up on pictures and talks. Were this prediction to come true, it would mean a tremendous stride towards barbarism. A better method of teaching youth not to think, of keeping it puerile, and of eventually boring it to death as well, could hardly be devised.

Just as barbarism can prevail in a society with a high degree of technical perfection, it may equally coincide with that other positive characteristic of modern society, universal education. To determine the level of culture from the degree of illiteracy is to deceive oneself with an outworn belief. A certain modicum of school knowledge in no way guarantees the possession of culture. It can hardly be called undue pessimism when, looking at the general state of mind of our time, one feels bound to speak in the following terms.

Delusion and misconception flourish everywhere. More than ever men seem to be slaves to a word, a motto, to kill one another with, to silence one another in the most literal sense. The world is filled with hate and misunderstanding. There is no way of measuring how great the percentage of the deluded is and whether it is greater than formerly, but delusion and folly have more power to harm and speak with greater authority. For the shallow, semi-educated person the beneficial restraints of respect for tradition, form and cult are gradually falling away. Worst of all is that widely prevalent indifference to truth which reaches its peak in the open advocacy of the political lie.

Barbarisation sets in when, in an old culture which once, in the course of many centuries, had raised itself to purity and clarity of thought and understanding, the vapours of the magic and fantastic rise up again from the seething brew of passions to cloud the understanding: when the *muthos* supplants the *logos*.

Again and again the new creed of the heroic will to power, with its exaltation of life over understanding, is seen to embody the very tendencies which to the believer in the Spirit spell the drift towards barbarism. For the "life-philosophy" does exactly this: it extols *muthos* over *logos*. To the prophets of the life-philosophy barbarism has no deprecatory implications. The term itself loses its meaning. The new rulers desire nothing else.

The gods of our time, mechanisation and organisation, have brought life and death. They have wired up the whole world, established contact throughout, created everywhere the possibility of co-operation, concentration of strength and mutual understanding. At the same time they have trapped the spirit, fettered it, stifled it. They have led man from individualism to collectivism. But with his unguided insight man has so far succeeded only in realising the evil that is in every collectivism, the negation of the deepest personal values, the slavery of the spirit. Will the future be one of ever greater mechanisation of society solely governed by the demands of utility and power?

Thus Oswald Spengler saw it when he posited the period of *Zivilisation* as the last phase of an outworn culture, a period in which all the earlier, living, organic values are replaced by exact control of the means of power and deliberate calculation of the desired effect. That the application of these means must lead a society to ruin leaves him cold by reason of his philosophical pessimism. Ruin is for him the inexorable fate of any culture.

Looking more deeply into Spengler's sombre vision one finds a number of inconsistencies which seem to impair its validity. In the first place, the standards by which he judges human action prove to be closely tied up with a certain romantic sentiment. His ideas of "greatness," "the will of the stronger," "sound instincts," "healthy warlike joy" (*kriegerische gesunde Freude*), "nordic heroism" and "Cæsarism of the Faustian world" have their roots in the soil of a naïve Romanticism. It is furthermore beyond dispute, I think, that the course of Western civilization during the seventeen years since Spengler's *Untergang des Abendlandes* first appeared, has definitely not been that of the ascendance of the type of *Zivilisation* as he developed it. For though it is true that society has been tending in this direction, that is, in the direction of greater technical control in the exercise of power and deliberate calculation of the desired effect, the type of human being has at the same time become ever more uncontrolled, more puerile, more susceptible to reactions of feeling. It is not the hard-bitten iron men of Spengler's conception who are ruling us to-day. One might perhaps put it this way: the world shows the aspect of Spengler's *Zivilisation* plus a measure of insanity, humbug and cruelty, coupled with sentimentality, which he did not foresee. For even his "noble animal," which he considers man to be, should be free of all this.

I have never quite understood why Spengler has chosen to name the modern human being of great spirit and high value after the dramatically not very impressive figure of Goethe's great dilogy: "Faustian culture, Faustian science, Faustian nations." But can one say of Faust that he was a predatory animal? Certainly that was not what Goethe meant him to be. Only a romantic vision can afford some justification for the application of the Faustian conception to the modern world.

On the whole there seem to be a good many reasons to prefer to call Spengler's *Zivilisation,* associated as it is with ferocity and humanity, "Barbarisation." Must we thereby share Spengler's fatalism? Is there no way out?

Seeking comfort, one involuntarily turns to the past. When one reviews the last two thousand years and distinguishes in them the historical units which we call civilizations, the periods of florescence appear always to have been relatively short. As far as our imperfect means of measurement seem to indicate, they seldom last more than two centuries. For the Greek civilization it is the fifth and fourth centuries B.C., for the Roman civilization the first century before and the first century after Christ (though here there is room for difference of opinion), for the Western-mediæval the twelfth and the thirteenth centuries, for Renaissance and Baroque the sixteenth and the seventeenth centuries. However vague and even arbitrary such delimitations must remain, the specific phases of highest development do not seem long. If we were to take the eighteenth and nineteenth centuries as the epoch of modern civilization, our time would appear to mark the end of the civilization we know, perhaps also the beginning of one which we do not know, one whose unfolding is still far distant. For there is no *"Le roi est mort, vive le roi"* about civilization.

They are but vain speculations, however, to which the contemplation of history has led us. Against all that seems to presage decline and ruin, contemporary humanity, except for a few fatalists, for once unanimously opposes the energetic declaration: but we *will* not perish. This world of ours is, with all its misery, too fine to allow it to sink into a night of human degradation and blindness of the spirit. We no longer count with an early end of all time. This heirloom of centuries called Western civilization has been entrusted to us to pass it on to coming generations, preserved, safeguarded, if possible enriched and improved, if it must be, impoverished, but at any rate as pure as it is in our power to keep it. Our faith in work, our belief in the possibility of salvation and the courage to promote it, none can take from us. We ask not who will reap the fruits of our labours. King Necho, Herodotus tells us, made an attempt to dig a canal through the isthmus between the Nile and the Red Sea. Messengers informed him that the work had already cost 120,000 lives and yet did not progress. The King consulted an oracle and the oracle spoke: "Thou labourest for the stranger." Whereupon the King dropped the project.—But if to-day a hundred oracles spoke their warning our decision would still be: *tant pis,* the work goes on.

Where lie the grounds for hope? Whence will deliverance come? What is needed to promote it?

The grounds for hope are of a very general nature, commonplace if you will. In every organism it is always the symptoms of disturbance, irregularity, and deterioration which attract most attention. The disease symptoms of our civilization manifest themselves very painfully and noisily. It is possible that in the great body of mankind the healthy flow of life nevertheless continues more powerfully than it would seem. The disease may work itself out.

In the great processes of nature and society, death-struggle and travail of birth seem to coincide. Always the new springs from the old. But the living do not know and cannot know what is the truly new that is destined to triumph.

Every great action is followed by reaction. If the reaction seems slow in coming one must remember to be patient with history. We are perhaps too inclined to believe that in our thoroughly organised and equipped society, with its articulation and conductivity, action and reaction are bound to follow one another more rapidly than formerly. The opposite may well be true. Just because the means for maintaining a given condition have increased enormously, the reaction takes longer to materialise. It is quite possible that later periods will view our own simply as the aftermath of the War.

History can predict nothing except that great changes in human relationships will never come about in the form in which they have been anticipated. We know that the shape of things to come will be different from any that we *can* imagine. In the outcome of any epoch there is always a component which is afterwards understood as the novel, the unexpected, the previously unthinkable. This unknown *may* mean ruin. But as long as expectation can hesitate between ruin and salvation it is our duty to hope.

It is indeed possible to distinguish certain signs suggesting that the unknown factor will be of a constructive nature. There are numerous tendencies which, regardless of all destructive forces, continue to work in the direction of a renewal and a reconstitution of civilization. Who could fail to see how in every field that is not directly affected by the evils of our time and even under the pressure of the latter, men in innumerable ways and with ever more perfect means are devoting themselves to the good of mankind? By building and making, by thinking and writing, by leading and serving, by caring and guarding. Or by simply living as the humble live, unconscious of the struggle for civilization. Unperturbed by folly and violence a vast number of men of good will quietly live on, with each building the future to the best of his ability. They barricade themselves as it were in a spiritual zone where the malevolence of time has no access and falsehood is not in repute. They do not become despondent and yield not to despair, however dark it may grow in their Emmaus.

Over the entire world a community is spread ready to accept the new, if it proves good, without abandoning all that is old and tested. They are not held together by banners and slogans, their fellowship is one of the spirit.

A striking sign of the pressure towards salvation is this: The nations have gone further in withdrawing themselves inside the shell of national sovereignty than ever before, some openly professing that they recognise nothing else. In more than one country internationalism has been officially proscribed. At the same time and just because of this rigid isolation of States the interplay of their relations is seen to be working itself out increasingly in the form of world politics. It is a world politics with the most defective means, with the most hair-raising evolutions—any moment may bring disaster—but a world politics none the less, an embryonic form of international collectivism which can no longer be evaded, which is forced into being in spite of everything—as if the necessity of concord over-rode all division and restrained every high-handedness.

If, then, there be reason for hope, whence is deliverance to come? "Progress," as such, will not bring it. We have progressed far enough in the ability to poison our world and our society. The progress of knowledge and applied science, however indispensable and inspiring, will not save our culture. Science and technology do not suffice as foundations of cultural life. The origins of the spiritual decay lie too deep for critical thought and the power of technical creation to be able of themselves to cure the ailment.

This leads us to a question which we have so far evaded: the connection between the cultural crisis and social-economic conditions. Many modern thinkers see the solution of the cultural problem as directly dependent on the social-economic question. It is not only the Marxist doctrinaires who hold this view. The influence of economic thought on our time has been so strong that many, without necessarily accepting the fundamental doctrines of Marxism, consider it beyond dispute that the spiritual ailment has its ultimate roots in the social-economic imperfections. This conviction is often associated with the belief that the far-reaching shifts and disturbances of a social-economic nature which we are witnessing afford proof that we are living in a period of fundamental structural change of society, "a period of reconstitution" ("*ein Zeitalter des Umbaus*"), as Karl Mannheim does not hesitate to call it. The indications of such a change are indeed impressive. After centuries of comparatively constant relationships a process of gradual disruption now seems to have attacked all that once seemed steady and solid in the field of production, exchange, standard of value, labour and government. The principles of private property and private enterprise seem to be shaking on their foundations. All this, it is said, indicates that we are moving towards a new and different construction of society.

Evidently this idea of structural change is largely based on the knowledge of historical parallels. Twice before, Western Europe has passed through a process of this kind: in the transitions from ancient to feudal society and from feudal to capitalist society. Neither of the two examples, however, is as useful for purposes of comparison as the almost inevitable simplification and condensation would make it appear. The process of feudalisation lasted for eight or nine centuries; it began in the time of the Roman Emperors and it was not completed until the eleventh century. The transition from feudal to bourgeois-capitalist society extends over a period from about 1100 to 1900, and the aggregate change is less intense than the current representation implies.

History offers no examples of a rapid change in fundamental relations such as is held to be taking place in our time. The two earlier structural changes were, moreover, less complete than that which is anticipated to-day. Both worked themselves out on the basis of an unchallenged principle of private property and hereditary devolution. All high civilizations of which we know (the State-communism of ancient Peru does not afford sufficiently conclusive evidence to the contrary) have in fact been based on these two foundations. From the historical point of view, therefore, the supposition of a rapid structural change of our society must be regarded as a bold hypothesis.

It may be argued that this alleged structural change will come about automatically and bring its own particular form of culture with it. This is the view of the old historical materialism. Most sociological and economic thinkers, however, consider our time incommensurable with earlier periods of supposedly more spontaneous growth in that to-day the insight into the problems, the conscious will to solve them and the means of solving them, are incomparably greater. The patient intends to cure himself. Can a society by its control of social forces carry out its will to reconstitution, lay out the road to such reconstitution, design and apply the means needed to achieve it? Many think it possible. "Planning" is the watchword of the day. It is held feasible to mechanise the processes of production, exchange, and consumption in such a way as to eliminate the individual springs of action. People conceive of a society in which competition and adventure will be suppressed, in which the individual self-interest will be transformed into a collective self-interest. Will such a condition of society also be one of culture?

Political science, however, expects more from planning than merely economic recovery. In wide circles a reconstruction of the organic form of society along the lines designed by well-considered thought is considered possible. As often as political life demands rejuvenation this old indispensable image of the State as an organism bears new fruit. A living conception of the State as an organism incorporates all the best notions of which we spoke in the attempt to define the concept of culture: balance, harmony, homogeneous striving, service, honour and loyalty. There is undoubtedly a profound desire for culture in the present nostalgic longing, especially noticeable in Germany, for rearrangement of the body politic in "estates" or living unities, natural ranks. A State which succeeded in elevating itself to an organism in which this noble service-relationship is realised, so that in his "estate" man felt himself in his proper place in society, would, in this way, have re-established at least a basis for culture.

This service-concept, however, would have to incorporate more than blind obedience to a power merely seeking to maintain and to strengthen itself in order to guarantee life and security to the community over which it rules. For true culture this kind of striving is not enough. A new spirit is required.

If, then, structural change and planning cannot promise a new spirit, will the Church bring it? Probably the Church will emerge purged and strengthened from the persecutions to which it is to-day subjected in more than one country. It is conceivable that one day Latin, Germanic, Anglo-Saxon and Slavonic religious spirit will meet and penetrate one another on the rock-bottom of Christianity in a world which also grasps the straightness of Islam and the depths of the East. The Churches as organisations, however, can only triumph in so far as they succeed in purifying the hearts of their members. Imposition of will or dictate will not turn the tide of evil.

XXI

KATHARSIS

It is not from intervention by social organisations that we must expect deliverance. The foundations of culture are not such that the organs of society, whether they be nations, churches, schools or parties, could reaffirm or strengthen them. What is required is an internal regeneration of the individual. The spiritual *habitus* of man himself will have to change.

The world of to-day has gone far on the road towards a universal disavowal of ethical standards. It no longer draws a clear line between good and evil. It is inclined to view the entire crisis of civilization as simply the conflict of opposing forces, a struggle for power between antagonists. And yet the one

231

and only hope lies in the recognition that in this struggle human action must be governed by a principle of absolute good and evil. From such recognition it follows that deliverance *cannot* lie in the triumph of one State, one people, one race, or one class. To subjugate the criteria of approval and condemnation to a purpose which is based on egotism is to pervert all true feelings of human responsibility.

The dilemma facing our time grows more acute every day. Once again look at the world in its present political confusion. Everywhere there are complications whose solution can hardly be evaded any longer, and of which any impartial observer must admit that a solution satisfying all legitimate interests and meeting all legitimate demands can hardly be devised. They concern problems of national minorities, impossible boundaries, prohibitions of natural unions, intolerable economic conditions. All these situations engender an atmosphere of exasperation which makes them into so many powder magazines threatening to blow off the lid at any moment. In every one of them the opposing interests are deadlocked in the conflict of rightful claims. There appear to be only two solutions. One of them is armed force, the other is adjustment on the basis of real international goodwill, of mutual renunciation of legitimate claims, of respect for the rights and interests of others; briefly, of unselfishness and equitableness.

From these virtues the world of to-day seems further removed than it has been, or at least pretended to be, for many a century. Even in principle the requirement of international equity and of international harmony to-day finds widespread disavowal. The theory of the unbridled authoritarian State provides an *a priori* acquittal for any potential invader. The world remains helplessly threatened by the madness of a devastating war bringing new and greater degeneration in its wake.

Public forces operate to ward off the senseless evil, to bring agreement and consultation. The smallest success of the League of Nations, though Ares greet it with a smirk of derision, to-day means more than the greatest display of power on land or at sea. Still, in the long run, the forces of a sensible internationalism are not enough if there is no change of spirit. Neither the prevention of war by international action nor the restoration of order and prosperity is in itself sufficient to bring a purification of culture. A new culture can only grow up in the soil of a purged humanity.

Katharsis: thus the Greeks called the state of mind produced by the spectacle of the tragedy, the stillness of heart in which compassion and fear have been dissolved, the purification of the soul which springs from having grasped a deeper meaning in things; which creates a grave and new preparedness for acts of duty and the acceptance of fate; which breaks the *hybris* as it was seen to be broken in the tragedy; which liberates from the violent passions of life and leads the soul to peace.

For the spiritual clarification which our time needs, a new *askesis* will be necessary. The bearers of a purified culture will have to be like those waking in an early dawn. They will have to shake off evil dreams. The dream of their soul which grew up out of the mud and would sink back into it. The dream of their brain which was but steel wire and their heart of glass. The dream of their hands growing into claws and the tusks between their lips. They will have to remind themselves that man can *will* himself not to be an animal.

The new *askesis* will not be one of renunciation of the world for heavenly bliss; it will be one of self-domination and tempered appraisal of power and pleasure. The exaltation of life will have to be toned down a little. One will have to remember how Plato already described the occupation of the wise man as a preparation for death. A steady orientation of the life-consciousness on death heightens the proper use of life itself.

The new *askesis* will have to be a surrender, a surrender to all that can be conceived as the highest. That can no more be nation or class than the individual existence of self. Happy those for whom that principle can only bear the name of Him who spoke: "I am the way, the truth, and the life."

The political revivalisms of the day have caught something of the spiritual attitude necessary for the restoration of culture, but it is impure, wrapped up in excessive puerilism, overborne by the cries of the caged animal, sullied by falsehood and deception. The younger generation, which will somehow have to carry on this culture in its next phase, is not lacking in readiness to give itself, to serve and to suffer, to do great deeds and to sacrifice itself. But the general weakening of judgment and the subversion of moral standards prevent it from testing the true worth of the principle which it is asked to serve.

It is difficult to see where the indispensable purification of the spirit will have to set in. Do we have to pass through still greater depths to become pliable? Or has the rallying of men of good will all over the world, unseen under the noisy confusion of the day, already begun? To repeat: the cultivation of internationalism is not all that is needed. None the less, it is of the greatest importance that this patient labour of preparing mankind for better times is continued, as it is carried on to-day in many places throughout the world, by small groups of like-minded individuals, by official international organisations, from the religious, political or cultural point of view. Wherever even the frailest flower of true internationalism (better were to call it international*ity*) raises its head, support it, strengthen it by grafting it on to the national consciousness, provided the latter be pure. It will flourish all the better for it. The international spirit—the word international itself already implies the preservation of nationalities, but of nationalities which tolerate each other and which do not make conflicts out of contrasts—may become the mould for the new ethics in which the opposition collectivism-individualism will have been dissolved. Is it an idle dream that one day this world could know such goodness? Even if it were, we would still have to cling to the ideal.

But does not the expression of these desires and expectations of a purging of the spirit, a katharsis which would be like a conversion, a rebirth, a regeneration, involve us in a contradiction with something we established in the beginning of this book? There we said that earlier periods, in their longing for a better society, had fixed their hopes on a reversal, an insight, a regaining of sense and virtue, as a conscious and early change for the better. Our time, however, knows that great spiritual and social changes are realised only through a process of gradual development, at the best temporarily accelerated by some extraordinary sudden impetus. And yet we are now demanding and hoping for a revulsion, in a way even for a return?

We are here faced again with the antinomic determination, the inconclusiveness of all our judgment. We are forced to recognise a certain amount of truth in the older vision. There must be a possibility of conversion and reversal in the development of civilization. We are thinking here of the recognition or retrieval of eternal truths, truths that are above the stream of evolution and change. It is these values that are at stake.

A time of heavy mental pressure such as that in which we are living is easier to bear for the old than the young. The old know that they only have to help carrying the burden of the times a little further. Resignedly they review how the world was, or seemed to be, when they began to shoulder their share of the burden, and what it appears to be turning into now. Their yesterday and to-morrow almost fade into one. Their fears and cares grow lighter in the proximity of death; their hope and trust, their will and courage to act, they place in the hands of those who have the task of living still before them. It is for the latter to accept the grave duty of judging, choosing, working, acting. Theirs the heavy responsibility, theirs the knowledge of what is to come.

KATHARSIS

The writer of these pages belongs to those whose privilege it is in their official occupations and personal life continually to remain in close contact with youth. It is his belief that the now young generation, in fitness for the difficult tasks of life, is fully equal to that which preceded it. The loosening of restraints, the confusion of thought, the diversion of attention and dissipation of energy under which this generation grew up have not made it weak, lax or indifferent. It seems open, generous, spontaneous, ready for pleasure but also for hardships; decisive, courageous and of great purpose. It walks with a lighter step than its predecessors.

To this young generation the task of ruling this world again as it would be ruled, to save it from perishing in pride and folly, to permeate it again with the spirit!

LINCOLN CHRISTIAN COLLEGE AND SEMINARY

EUROPEAN HISTORY TITLES IN
NORTON PAPERBOUND EDITIONS

Aron, Raymond. *On War.* N107

Aron, Raymond. *The Opium of the Intellectuals.* N106

Benda, Julien. *The Treason of the Intellectuals.* N470

Bloch, Marc. *Strange Defeat: A Statement of Evidence Written in 1940.* N371

Brandt, Conrad. *Stalin's Failure in China.* N352

Brinton, Crane. *The Lives of Talleyrand.* N188

Butterfield, Herbert. *The Whig Interpretation of History.* N318

Burn, W. L. *The Age of Equipoise.* N319

Calleo, David P. *Europe's Future: The Grand Alternatives.* N406

Dehio, Ludwig. *Germany and World Politics in the Twentieth Century.* N391

East, W. Gordon. *The Geography Behind History.* N419

Eyck, Erich. *Bismarck and the German Empire.* N235

Ferrero, Guglielmo. *The Reconstruction of Europe.* N208

Feis, Herbert. *Contest Over Japan.* N466

Feis, Herbert. *Europe: The World's Banker 1870-1914.* N327

Feis, Herbert. *The Spanish Story.* N339

Feis, Herbert. *Three International Episodes: Seen from E. A.* N351

Fischer, Fritz. *Germany's Aims in the First World War.*

Gatzke, Hans W. *Stresemann and the Rearmament of Germany.* N486

Gulick, Edward Vose. *Europe's Classical Balance of Power.* N413

Halperin, S. William. *Germany Tried Democracy.* N280

Hobsbawm, E. J. *Primitive Rebels.* N328

Langer, William L. *Our Vichy Gamble.* N379

May, Arthur J. *The Hapsburg Monarchy: 1867- 1914.* N460

Menéndez Pidal, Ramón. *The Spaniards in Their History.* N353

Newhouse, John. *Collision in Brussels: The Common Market Crisis of 30 June 1965.*

Nichols, J. Alden. *Germany After Bismarck: The Caprivi Era, 1890-1894.* N463

Rowse, A. L. *Appeasement.* N139

Russell, Bertrand. *Freedom versus Organization: 1814-1914.* N136

Thompson, J. M. *Louis Napoleon and the Second Empire.* N403

Waite, Robert G. L. *Vanguard of Nazism: The Free Corps Movement in Postwar Germany, 1918-1923.* N181

Whyte, A. J. *The Evolution of Modern Italy.* N298

Wolfers, Arnold. *Britain and France between Two Wars.* N343

Wolf, John B. *Louis XIV.*

Wolff, Robert Lee. *The Balkans in Our Time.* N395